Wise and Wonderful

Life Lesson for Single Mothers
Fourth Edition

C. Chérie Hardy

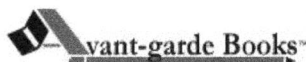

Avant-garde Books™

Avant-garde Books
Spiritual Division
Post Office Box 566
Mableton, Georgia 30126
www.avantgardebooks.net

Wise and Wonderful
Life Lessons for Single Mothers
Fourth Edition

ISBN: 978-0-9743676-7-5

This book is dedicated to:

Latasha Edwards

"The wise woman builds her house, but the foolish pulls it down with her hands."-Proverbs 14:1 (NKJV)

Wise and Wonderful
Life Lessons for Single Mothers

C. Chérie Hardy

Table of Contents

Wise and Wonderful
Life Lessons for Single Mothers

C. Chérie Hardy

Table of Contents

*Adapted from *Love Doesn't Hurt: Life Lessons for Women*. Copyright © 2012 by C. Chérie Hardy

Wise and Wonderful
Life Lessons for Single Mothers

C. Chérie Hardy

A Daughter's Love

"There isn't a relationship in a family that is more important than the relationship a child has with her mother, or someone in that role, and we have to value that."
–Michelle Obama

A woman can never know what it's like to be a mother until she becomes one. Yet, we all know it's not an easy task, especially when done single-handedly. However, I happened to have one of those mothers who made parenting look effortless as a child. Now that I've grown into a young adult, I have a better understanding of what it really took for my mother to raise a little girl all by herself.

My extended family was always generous with helping to provide my needs, but for the most part, it was my mother who built my character, fed me wisdom, demonstrated patience, encouraged me, and made many sacrifices (both personal and financial) on my behalf. It's important for children to know and understand the mother who provides for them and loves them unconditionally. I feel so blessed to have never doubted my mother's love. At times, in the essence of my naïveté and ignorance, I didn't understand why my mother made certain choices. Now, having responsibilities of my own, I have learned that one choice can change your life forever so I began to value and appreciate the choices my mother made while thinking of my well-being.

College exposed me to people who grew up in homes much different from my own. Leaving home allowed me to get an inside scoop of the interaction between mothers and their daughters—especially those that contrast my mother and me. This led to a deeper appreciation for all that my mother had done for me. Since I was always raised to be grateful, I learned to thank God even more for the mother He had given me.

Ultimately, I learned that there is no specific age in which a child is one hundred percent independent of his/her parent. Each child goes through various stages of responsibility that act as stepping stones to adulthood. However, as children we continually remain interdependent to our families and communities. In other words, children always need their parents regardless of their age. The love, encouragement, and accountability we get from our parents fortify us during our lifetime.

As a mother, the impact you have on your children's lives can either make or break them. Attempting to control and dominate your children is never a good thing. However, positive guidance and character reinforcement in the right direction are always beneficial. I have witnessed parents who missed opportunities to become closer to their children because they continually tried to be dictators, instead of loving, spiritual coaches in their children's lives.

I hope that this God-inspired book, *Wise and Wonderful: Life Lessons for Single Mothers* can be a guide for every woman parenting alone. A comforting afterthought that being a single parent is not the end of the road or a curse to society's revered ideal of the nuclear family. For a child to have even one loving and sane parent in this world is a blessing. If that parent remains wise and wonderful despite the hardships and strains of life, she is giving the world a precious gift—an example of perseverance, strength, and faith.

For the most part children understand when their parent argues, "I'm doing what's best" and "one day you will understand." But there is a point when making decisions for your child translates into trying to live your child's life. This can cause resentment and a broken home. At some point when parents know that they have done all they can, it is time to let go. Children will learn through their own understanding and experiences. We are always listening even when it seems as if we are not. We never forget what our mothers shout or whisper to us.

Moreover, when children feel as though their mother genuinely has love and concern for them, their words of wisdom shall never leave them, no matter what; they are embedded into their hearts forever. The same is true when a mother brands her children with negative and discouraging words; they leave an indelible and painful scar on a child's soul.

Therefore, the goal as a parent, specifically a mother, is to not dominate, demean, or neglect, but to nurture, love, protect, guide and support. Consider parenting not necessarily a job, but a gift. At the end of the day, every mother needs to ask herself, despite the mistakes my children make, as well as, differences in character and personality, did I love and accept them anyway. How fortunate I am that I can truly say my mother has done all of that and more. I love her deeply and feel eternally grateful for God blessing me with the woman I call, "mother".

Hopefully, this book will be a helpful tool that single mothers can use as they raise their children alone because it is undeniably no easy task. I highly recommend that you note the life lessons of the author, not merely because she is my mother, but because I (and thousands of children she has taught) have directly experienced and benefited from her wisdom and instruction. I am a witness that what she believes is beneficial and true.

Felicia C. Hardy, Daughter of Author

Letter to Single Mothers

"If any of you lacks wisdom, he [or she] should ask God, who gives generously to all without finding fault, and it will be given to him. But when he [or she] asks, he must believe and not doubt because he who doubts is like a wave of the sea, blown and tossed by the wind."
–James 1:5-6 (NIV)

Reflection Questions

1. What memories are you creating for your children?
2. What actions have you taken to become an effective mother?
3. With whom do you spend your quality time? (co-workers, a man, your children, …)
4. Do you believe parenting involves doing what comes naturally?

Dear Beloved Single Mother,

I hope that you realize how honored you are by God. God is an advocate for the fatherless. While your children might not have a biological father in their lives, they are blessed with a Heavenly Father who can supply all of their needs and so much more. It is important for you, as the leader of the home, to direct your children to God's perfection instead of a man's weaknesses and flaws. Don't let them internalize negative statistics about single-parent homes. Remind them that there are countless, successful, and healthy people who didn't grow up in a home with a father. Your children are blessed and highly favored because they belong to God!

It's important for you to guard your mind and heart because although motherhood is an honored gift from God, it remains one of the hardest jobs on the planet. This noble title and position in a woman's life demands one of the highest levels of personal accountability. I am sure that you have already discovered that motherhood is incomparable to any other responsibility a woman might ever have.

Even with a loving and valiant man at a woman's side, the duties of motherhood can seem frightening, overwhelming, and frustrating. **Everything a mother thinks, does, and says has a direct impact on the quality of her children's lives. Mothers lay an important foundation that will create an indelible mark on their children's minds and hearts.** Mothers are so powerful that whatever they teach their children determines the state of our world.

Therefore, one of the greatest legacies a woman can leave is being an example of good character and strength for her children. **This is accomplished when mothers let God — the Creator of the Universe, be the principal guiding force for everything they do.**

The primary objective of this book is not necessarily to tell you what you should do as a mother. Simply put, there is no universal blueprint for parenting. Effective parenting is a complex endeavor and continuous adjustments must be made in order to accommodate each individual child throughout his/her life. Even though all children are wired with common traits as human beings, no child is exactly like another one.

What I hope to accomplish through this literary work is motivating women to think about how our actions as mothers impact our children. **A woman can only grow as a mother when she is willing to continually assess her own actions and beliefs.** More importantly, she must have the courage to take ownership of the state of her family's health. She must also be willing to modify her attitude and behavior if necessary to support the development of herself and her children.

Additionally, she must accept God's truth and let it direct her actions. This is not always easy because bad habits are hard to break, and change is one of the most difficult actions for humans to embrace. **However, with God all things are possible.**

I have learned much about children as an educator and mother for almost 30 years. It is with great respect and love that I candidly share some of the insight I have gained. I don't define myself as an expert. I recognize there is so much more to learn. I just humbly submit myself as a student of children; they can teach us so much if we would give them the right kind of attention and unconditional love.

It is my prayer that every reader will be inspired, encouraged, and enlightened to be the mother God predestined her to be. It is God who entrusts women with this divine opportunity to shape His world — only a woman can carry and birth a human being, thus creating a powerful spiritual and emotional tie between mother and child; the effects of this special bond have the potential to influence lives even beyond death. The state as well as strength of this important maternal, connection are not determined by a woman's education, marital status, history, or socioeconomic circumstances, but instead measured by the love (or lack of love) that a mother demonstrates to her children.

Precious daughter of God, give up your exhaustive efforts to raise your children alone. Don't overwhelm your mind with trying to figure out how every problem will be solved and why certain issues exist. Seek God with your whole heart. Submit yourself to His will. He will begin to reveal that all pain has a purpose; every obstacle presents an opportunity; and every tragedy can lead to triumph if you just trust in Him.

Motherhood becomes the most rewarding experience in the world when you surrender to God. With both your spiritual and physical eyes, you have the pleasure of watching your children become gifts to humanity. Strengthen your effectiveness as a mother by communicating with God about your concerns, hopes and needs. Instead of going to your telephone to nag family and friends, go to the Throne of God who cares for you more than any other human being.

Blessed single mother, believe that our generous and compassionate God is willing and able to provide for you and your children. Let God instruct you on how to nurture and recognize the unique gifts in your children. Permit Him to teach you the methods you should implement to develop their character. Let God be the Ultimate Authority in your life and show you how to become *wise and wonderful*.

In His Service,

C. Chérie Hardy

Chapter One
Favor for the Fatherless

"A father of the fatherless, a defender of widows, is God in His holy habitation."-Psalm 68:5 (NKJV)

Reflection Questions

1. Do you believe that your child is doomed to fail because he or she is growing up without a father?

2. Do you communicate that your child can only have things based on his or her biological father's participation and provision?

3. How do you teach your children not to internalize negative stereotypes, proclamations and declarations connected to growing up in a single-parent home?

One of the most powerful lessons I've learned throughout my life is that what I believe is powerful enough to determine outcomes. That's why it is paramount that as a single mother you guard your thoughts concerning the quality of life that you *believe* your children can have. Every day you must affirm to yourself and your children that God favors the fatherless, and that He is greater than any man. There should be no doubt in your heart that God is more than willing and able to take care of you and your children. This will only become your reality when you believe. On the other hand, if you are plagued with thoughts that your children are doomed to suffer because they lack a father, you will create so many disadvantages for them. This doesn't have to happen.

The first, and most important step to becoming an effective, single mother is believing that God loves your children more than any human being can, including you. Of course, it was not His original blueprint for the family that children should grow up in a home without a righteous man to protect and provide for them. And, it grieves God's heart when a man dies or he abdicates his paternal responsibilities. Nevertheless, God deeply cares for children. Since the genesis of humankind, God has blessed fatherless children. He has used them as examples of His grace and omnipotence. Millions of people throughout history have become successful despite not having a father in their homes. God understands more than we do that children don't need a father, they need a GOOD one. The truth is that even the most loving man in the world could never be a better father than He can.

Beloved single mother, you must believe that children will do well with God as their shepherd. Whenever, you are tempted to succumb to the negative stereotypes about single-parent homes, you must draw closer to God and pray for his guidance, protection, and provision. I, like so many other single mothers, am a witness that our loving Heavenly Father will neither leave nor forsake you and your children. The key is believing the truth, and not the lies often propagandized in the media.

Be mindful of the voices that you allow to influence you. Instead of internalizing negative declarations about children from single-parent homes, meditate on the Psalmist's proclamation: "When my father and my mother forsake me, then the LORD will take care of me."-Psalm 27: 10 (NKJV)

Lean on God and you will discover that He will make sure your children have just as much or more than those who have a father. Your precious ones will achieve greatness and be positive agents of change when you teach them to trust in God's faithfulness.

Chapter Two
Unconditional Love: The Greatest Gift to Children

"What's the best parenting strategy for all children? It is unconditional love!" –Felicia C. Hardy

Reflection Questions

1. How do you demonstrate unconditional love to your children?

2. Do you verbally communicate that you love your children?

3. Is what you do for your children (or to them) dependent upon a condition such as appearance, behavior, levels of achievement, etc.?

Love is the greatest and most essential gift that a mother can give her children. Love cannot be lost, not even by death; it cannot be torn apart; it cannot rust or decay; and it is not dependent upon conditions. The good news is that love does not cost and it is guaranteed to give children a strong sense of self-worth and confidence. It is love that empowers them to endure and overcome the difficult seasons of their lives.

When children make mistakes, which they will inevitably do often, it is love that inspires them to get up again. It is love that helps them to hold and keep their heads up when they make mistakes. Love gives human beings the courage to choose purpose over peer-pressure and constructive activities instead of destructive habits, like drug and alcohol abuse. When children get love from their mothers, they are less likely to search for it in dangerous places and people.

When a mother loves her children, they will know it through her actions and words because real love cannot be shut up in a person's heart. In other words, a mother cannot truly love her children and fail to say it. Some might argue that some people find it difficult to verbally communicate their feelings. However, I believe it's impossible to genuinely love people and never tell them. Just as a woman can profess her love to a man, it should be easier for that same woman to articulate love to her children who are extensions of herself. Simply put, love cannot be contained! Love is so explosive that it becomes like an active volcano and eventually erupts.

What is the origin of love? Love comes from a preternatural source — God, the Creator of the Universe. When we connect with Him, we discover unconditional love. This connection makes us a human conduit for it. Thus, while love comes *from* God, it manifests itself *through* us.

Therefore, it is imperative for all mothers, particularly women who are raising children alone, to establish and/or strengthen a relationship with God. The weaker the connection with God, the less likely a woman can show unconditional love to her children. Through a relationship with God, mothers learn that their children should be treated as blessings, not burdens; they should be celebrated and not merely tolerated.

When God is directing our paths, we get the perfect prescription for addressing our children's needs. After all, our children come from Him. They are His one-of-a-kind priceless masterpieces. We must never forget that we are stewards of His precious property. Our principal goal as mothers should be raising our children to be pleasing to their Heavenly Father — to bear witness of His glory. They belong to Him, but He has entrusted us with the responsibility of teaching them to become reflections of Him, and His character.

11

The parenting strategies I share throughout this book are God-centered. I feel enormously blessed to have worked with children as an educator and mother for almost 30 years. My experiences have led me to conclude that when children grow up with a healthy understanding of God and what He desires for their lives, they are more successful than those who don't get this instruction. A relationship with God empowers them to overcome obstacles and difficult situations.

While it is inevitable that all people make mistakes, children who embrace a loving, forgiving, and merciful God are more likely to triumph over their troubles. Being a child in the 21st century poses many challenges that deal with self-identity and worth. It seems to be an era when the world has become cruel and intolerant of those who don't fit into a narrow scope of so-called beauty and "coolness" or adhere to a distorted view of what is right.

The revelation of God's love becomes a powerful tool for helping children navigate through difficult times such as adolescence. God, unlike what is promoted in the mainstream media, wants children to embrace their uniqueness and feel loved just as they are. He doesn't exclude them and His unconditional acceptance of them is more valuable than anything they could ever experience from a human being.

I cannot count how many times that I have witnessed children being unfazed by rejection at school because they knew how much they were loved by their family members, and by God. On the other hand, I have seen countless children emotionally and socially devastated because they feel unloved and unwanted by their parents. The neglect and rejection at home only exacerbates their problems at school. These children often suffer from depression and in the worst cases, see suicide as the only escape from their pain.

It is imperative for mothers to give their children the same treatment that they want for themselves. Some people have the mentality that their children are like servants or worse, slaves. They misuse their position of authority to control their children for their own selfish desires. They constantly bark out commands and insults, in addition to, physically and emotionally abusing their children. They also allow others to abuse their children unchecked, yet they seem surprised when they children choose to distance themselves the first chance they get.

This doesn't have to happen. Healing and restoration are possible for any family, but it takes hard work. It starts with four life-changing actions. First, mothers must seek God for direction and guidance. This starts with prayer which I expound upon in the next chapter. God is an advocate for the fatherless and He desires that we lean on Him for provision and wisdom. Everyday a mother should petition God (pray) for help on how to raise her children. She must plug in her spiritual antennae to hear from God and make adjustments in her own behavior to help her children.

Secondly, mothers need to assess the state of their families. Until children can take care of themselves, they are dependent upon their parents. The primary source of some children's problems is their own home. Mothers must ask God to search their hearts and accept that their mistakes directly affect their children's welfare. They must also seek God for the strength and courage to make changes when necessary.

"Search me, O God, and know my heart; try me and know my thoughts; and see if there be any wicked way in me and lead me in the way everlasting." –Psalm 139:23-24 (KJV)

Not only is God pleased when a mother corrects her mistakes, but her children will respect and cherish her even more. Again, this is only possible when God is directing a mother's mind and heart. The bottom line is trying to love children without God is like attempting to make a cake without flour. It is a recipe for a disastrous home that will lead to chaos, confusion, and resentment.

Thirdly, mothers need to never forget that their children as extensions of themselves. A positive change of attitude improves outcomes. God specializes in transforming minds and hearts. Good mothers decide to give their children the same respect, love, forgiveness, mercy, support, etc. that they need and desire for themselves. When a mother acts on God's truth instead of negative distortions, she will see her children as precious blessings from God; she will not abuse, neglect, and reject them. She will treat her children exactly the way she expects to be treated.

If a mother wants patience, she should be patient with her children. If she desires mercy and forgiveness for her own life, it should be easy to pass them on to her children. And the same unconditional love she wants for herself must be planted in her precious children. **The title of "mother" doesn't give a woman the right to do and say anything to her children.**

I know a woman who felt that it was her divine right to say and do whatever she wanted to her children. She expected them to take her abuse and cruelty without protest. Any of her children who complained about her actions or expressed concerns, was considered rebellious, disrespectful, and evil. **However, the truth is that it is a woman's divine responsibility to respect, protect, and provide for her children. Most importantly, mothers are required by God to love their children. He expects mothers to be reflections of Him.**

Fourthly, mothers need to seek out ways to heal their minds and bodies, especially from broken relationships. Mothers can only give their children what they possess themselves. If mothers are sick, fatigued, spiritually broken,

14

and weary, how can they give their best to their children? Whatever a mother lacks, her children will not have. Many single mothers are overwhelmed with having no or limited financial and parental support from the absent father. Furthermore, they are hurting from failed relationships.

The good news is that motherhood becomes joyful when women decide to become strong in the Lord and the power of His might. When a mother's faith is unwavering, she will trust that God will supply all her (and her children's) needs. A strong connection with God allows a mother to envision her children becoming success stories instead of tragedies. It helps her to believe that God compensates for her human limitations and will supernaturally work out things on her behalf.

As mothers, when our troubles are magnified within us, destructive behavior towards our children can be manifested outwardly. If we don't depend on God as single mothers, we may find ourselves doing some abhorrent thing in an effort to escape our painful reality. We might unintentionally hurt our children and produce the spirit of anger and rebellion in our homes.

Dearest sister, becoming a mother your children will celebrate and revere involves purposely seeking out people, places, and information that teach you about what has consistently worked for millions of mothers throughout history. Rather than judge yourself as a good or bad mother, learn how to judge the strategies you employ as a parent. Let God do a spiritual inventory and evaluation of what you are doing.

Is what you're doing effective or ineffective? Are your children's lives being enhanced by your parenting methods, or are their lives getting worse? Is family life chaotic or peaceful? A single mother is the head and leader of the household. She has the power to determine the quality of her children's lives.

When a mother is strong, her children will reap the rewards of her strength. The same is true for the opposite. If a mother is weak, she is incapable of teaching her children how to engage in victorious living.

Despite how difficult life may be, every mother has an opportunity to become wise and wonderful. In fact, the negative events you've experienced can act as catalysts for positive change. Regardless of your past or present condition, God is willing and able to heal, deliver, redeem, and set free anyone in spiritual bondage. His way, the only way, leads to eternal peace, joy, success, etc. Unlike most things in life, you don't need money to have a relationship with God. Furthermore, coming to Him has no negative side effects and is free of dangerous risks and complications.

Awesome mother, become wise and wonderful by recognizing that your children are blessings from God to be cherished and appreciated. **Establishing and/or strengthening your relationship with Our Creator will allow you to love your children as He does. Ultimately, your walk with Him will lead you to become an effective mother that your children will call honorable.**

Do not let another second pass without humbly and sincerely asking God to reveal Himself to you. If you feel that you already have a relationship with Him, pray for a higher level of intimacy and understanding. Petition God to teach you how to be the good steward of the children with whom He has blessed you. Let the love that emanates from Him guide what you think, do, and say.

"Love is patient and kind. It does not envy, it does not boast, it is not proud. It does not dishonor others, it is not self-seeking, it is not easily angered, and it keeps no record of wrongs. Love does not delight in evil but rejoices with the truth. It always protects, always trusts, always hopes, and always perseveres.

Love never fails. But where there are prophecies, they will cease; where there are tongues, they will be stilled; where there is knowledge, it will pass away." –I Corinthians 13:4-8 (NIV)

Chapter Three
Watch and Pray

"Do not be anxious about anything, but in everything by prayer and petition, with thanksgiving, present your requests to God." (Philippians 4:6 NIV)

Reflection Questions

1. With whom do you discuss your children? (God, your friends, family members...?)

2. Do you regularly pray for your children?

3. How do you determine what are the best solutions to problems concerning your children?

Being an effective mother, involves much more than getting children to meet our personal expectations and making them do what *we* want. One of the most important roles of a parent is to build character. It is ultimately character that will protect our children from unnecessary disappointment and hardship. Character allows them to keep what they earn throughout their lives; it helps them use the natural gifts endowed by God in ways that benefit mankind.

Therefore, it is paramount that as mothers we watch and fervently pray for our children without ceasing. Moreover, we must let God's plans guide us on what values to inculcate in our children — which lessons to teach that will save them rather than those that cause unnecessary pain, suffering, and pre-mature death. This can be quite difficult for mothers who are parenting alone. The parenting techniques that are the quickest and easiest are generally not the most useful for shaping children with good character.

However, talking to God about our children is one of the most effective parenting strategies that we can employ. After all, our children come from Him. It is imperative that we consult Him on a regular basis about what's best for them. It is God who has placed children in our stewardship. Therefore, we need to seek Him out because He knows our children better than anyone. He is the Divine Manufacturer and Creator of all things. It is He who wired each child with his/her inherent gifts, personality, and physical attributes, just as He made us, the mothers charged with tenderly caring for His property.

God is the best person to talk to (pray) about what is happening in our children's lives because His omniscience allows Him to see things about them that we don't and cannot. If we submit to God's authority, He will guide us and equip us with the tools to prepare our children for His purpose.

Blessed mother, you cannot get instructions about what you should do for your children without communicating with God. Each day, regardless of how overloaded your schedule may be, you must set aside time to talk (pray) to Him. Prayer allows you to express your gratitude; release your concerns; ask for wisdom and solutions; and get revelation about things you don't understand. Moreover, when you *pray*, your children won't become *prey* to our spiritual enemy who seeks to destroy them.

Throughout your day, mental prayers will strengthen you. **However, from this day forward, make a personal commitment to get DEEP (Drop Everything and Enter Prayer), and engage in intensive communication with God.** The bottom line is that if you don't get spiritual nutrition from God, you won't be able to complete your to-do list anyway. When God manages a mother's life, she can manage hers, and minimize the negative effects of stress. God gives mothers supernatural power and strength to handle parenting.

Prayer also gives mothers peace concerning their children's welfare. It's hard not to internalize the terror reported in the newspapers. Mothers often agonize about their children getting hurt, sick or dying. The emotion of fear can be an ever, present force looming over a mother's mind. With prayer, mothers learn that even if they struggle with the emotion of fear, it doesn't have to dominate their lives and prevent them from releasing their children to God.

Who is a better authority than God to help your children fulfill His divine plan for their lives? No one! Think about the mother of Dr. Benjamin Carson, one of the world's leading pediatric neurosurgeons. She was uneducated and poor, but knew the power of prayer. As she struggled with single parenting, she petitioned God for help on what to do about her two sons. God gave her clear answers on what adjustments she needed to make in her household in order to, redirect the destructive path her sons were taking. Instead of Dr. Carson becoming a negative statistic, he became a world-renown doctor lauded for saving children's lives as a surgeon. Today, Dr. Carson and his brother lead extraordinary lives because they had a praying mother! Yes, prayers change outcomes and transform lives!

Never forget that God supersedes problems and disadvantaged circumstances. The children you intercede for in prayer will become great blessings to you. God hears the passionate cries of mothers without regard of their native language. You don't have to be the most eloquent and/or articulate speaker in order to talk to Him. And, no specific format to prayer is necessary. If you are deaf and cannot use your tongue, God interprets the language of your heart; He relishes the sincerity of your inner voice. God knows when you possess a deep yearning for His presence.

Make a decision at this moment that you will no longer give God an exhausted sigh before closing you through tough times.

If you choose to pray at night, I recommend that you pray with your children first before going to God's throne alone. Tuck your little ones in, read them a bedtime story, kiss them, and say something sweet. For older children, always say something positive and encouraging before they go to bed. Of course, they will never get too old to hear the words, "I love you."

When your home is quiet and all you hear is the steady hum of a refrigerator or air conditioner, you have gotten *deep*. Affirm aloud that nothing will separate you from the love of God. Praise and worship God for who He is: the omnipotent creator of everything.

Believe in your heart that despite how disheartening situations may appear, God always works things out for His glory. Thank God in advance for letting you see and experience in your heart the manifestation of His power and presence. Thank Him for protecting your children and providing their needs.

Never doubt that God doesn't hear your thoughts. Be prepared and ready to receive revelation and guidance from God as He gently whispers wisdom to your heart. There is so much wisdom and love He wants to instill in you!

Throughout my daughter's life, I have prayed for God to guide me on how to deal with challenging situations. I have learned that my response to problems can have a tremendous influence on what my child believes. One of many personal examples that illustrate my point is when my daughter came home from elementary school distressed about peer pressure, teasing, teachers, etc. Of course, I did exactly what I am encouraging you to do. I went to God for answers. I stayed in prayer.

It started when we first relocated to Georgia. While we both endured a stressful transitional period, it was harder for my daughter who was only eight years old at the time. At school, she became the "new kid" from Florida who was different. Almost daily, she was teased about her non-designer clothing and kinky hair.

Prior to this time, we hadn't given much thought to brand name clothing, shoes, etc. We weren't materialistic and I had always believed that a person makes the clothing; the clothing doesn't make a person. My beautiful daughter went to school looking nice but the name on the tag didn't matter very much.

As I watched my daughter's attitude about her self-image start to waver, I sought God for wisdom about how to respond. He put the words in my mouth and I began to teach my child that no matter how expensive her clothing was and how neat her hair was coiffed, there would always be someone finding fault and pointing out some perceived imperfection. She learned that people with feelings of low self-worth often put others down and resort to name-calling in order to make themselves feel better. I taught her to never compare herself with anyone else. Moreover, we resolved that competing with oneself was less exhausting than trying to outdo others to be "the so-called best."

There were many life lessons from God that I would pass along. However, some were addressed sooner than I had expected. I also used this time to teach my daughter how to distinguish the difference between the symbols of wealth and real wealth. Furthermore, I let her know that her hair was created by God and if anyone had a problem with it, he/she should consult Him. She could change her hair, but it wouldn't mean people would stop harassing her about it.

Through this continual coaching, my child became more confident about who she was born to be. When she was given a shopping allowance, she only bought name brand items on sale, not because she thought the clothing would make her a better person, but because she liked them. She became comfortable in her own skin; she was transformed into a leader at school whom her peers admired and respected.

It was prayer with righteous actions that determined outcomes! Talking to God determined if my child would be confident or uncomfortable with herself. Whatever wisdom God gives to you, you are able to pass on to your children. However, you can only give them what you yourself own and possess. So as God taught me, I practiced whatever I shared with my child. Through God's anointing, I became a model of inner strength for her to emulate. In other words, I became a better woman and mother, as I instilled certain values that I passed on. I also evolved into a more confident woman as I faced my own struggles with self-image.

The church, schools and society are not the ultimate authorities on determining what your child will become. It is up to you, the mother (single or not), to train up your children with the tools to live in this world with dignity and positive values. Prayer gives you power to look beyond your circumstances and see hope in God's wisdom.

This is why that I highly recommend that you make sure that prayer is first on your to-do list. With intimate fellowship with God, you're able to accomplish important goals. Be encouraged regardless of how bad things may appear. God has a solution to every problem you face. While the expression, "Prayer changes things" sounds like a cliché, it is true! Unlike family members and friends, God is available 24 hours a day. Your secrets are safe. Furthermore, God eagerly wants you to embrace His principles so that you can receive His promises.

Never forget that prayer is a vital response to coping with your own personal challenges, including those connected to single parenthood. It is the most important act you can do for strength, peace, guidance, and joy. Prayer enables mothers to inherit special treasures from God which later become spiritual heirlooms to their children.

Finally, keep in mind that prayer doesn't only involve you talking to God. It also means you must be still and allow Him to speak to your heart. His voice and direction become clear the more you fellowship with Him—the greater your desire to know Him, not just for what you can get, but for who you can become through His power. Learn to get quiet during prayer time and listen intently for His wisdom. He loves you and your children more than you will ever comprehend. He has so much to tell you. Open your heart in prayer and receive answers from the Most High God. He will answer your prayers according to His perfect will. Cast your cares upon Him and rest knowing that He will never fail to help you.

"...The effectual fervent prayer of a righteous man [or woman] availeth much." --James 5:16b (KJV)

Chapter Four
Lead by Example

"Psychologists will attest that parents can program their children for joy and achievement with the words they share and the example they set." (Angela Burt-Murray)

Reflection Questions

1. What examples are you setting for your children?
2. Do your children see you as a woman of honor?
3. Are you willing to change your behavior and adjust your attitude if necessary to become a better mother?

When I was around fourteen years old, I watched my mother graduate from college with honors. After giving birth to four children, she made a decision to complete the post-secondary education she had started before I was born. I remember this being one of the proudest moments of my childhood.

Today I realize my mother's powerful example of returning to school, even against the odds, inspired me to endure my own difficult college days. My mother modeled for my sisters and me, not only the value of getting an education, but also the importance of finishing what you start, as well as, how hard work pays off. I believe in my heart that my mother's example of resilience and perseverance attributed to all four of her children becoming college graduates.

To be effective mothers, we don't have to be perfect. However, we should do everything in our power to give our children a model of how to live with integrity in spite of our imperfections and mistakes. **As mothers, we are our**

children's first and most influential teachers. Our children are constantly observing our behavior even when we think they are not; they will subconsciously emulate our conduct even if we try to convince them not to. As mothers, we need to be our best so that our children can be. They benefit from our good choices, but suffer and become casualties of unrighteous living.

"He who walks with the wise grows wise, but a companion of fools suffers harm." –Proverbs 13:20 (NIV)

A single mother is the heart of her family. She creates the ambience of her home. Her decisions, thoughts, and values as well as words, directly impact her children's behavior. To operate as an honorable mother, she cannot neglect investing in the resources that will nurture her mind, body, and spirit. She must also be willing to admit her shortcomings and adjust her behavior if necessary to enhance the health of her family. This will teach children how to take ownership of their mistakes.

Unfortunately, some women believe that motherhood is synonymous with "making children behave". They attempt to do this by constantly barking out directives and criticizing children when they make mistakes. However, domination and control are adversaries of righteous parenting. Effective parenting involves teaching "how to", which involves good examples, not just telling your children what to do. In other words, mothers must be willing model the same behavior they expect from their children.

A good mother inculcates values which come from God. Later, through her actions, she becomes a living example of how to implement and practice the lessons she taught. It is evitable though that all mothers will make mistakes. However, a mother's mistakes can be used to teach powerful lessons about recovery and correction.

Although extended family members will have a significant influence on your children's lives, you are the primary leader and adult role model of your household. Your job is not just to tell children what they do wrong, but offer reasonable and clear solutions to changing their behavior; you are charged with *showing* them how to solve their own problems.

Train a child in the way he should go, and when he is old he will not turn from it." (Proverbs 22:6 NKJV)

Never forget that your children came through your womb, but they were conceived in God's heart. They are not your property to make as your personal slaves to fulfill your will; they are not clones of you and may not share your goals and aspirations. Your children are gifts from the Creator of the Universe to be cherished and loved—just as they are. As a mother, you are the steward assigned by God to raise your children with the tools to operate as blessings on Earth.

The strength of your relationship with God will determine the basis of the quality of your personal interaction with each of your children. It is crucial that you use your limited time with them wisely. They will be grown and soaring from "the nest" sooner than you think. Keep this in mind when you are raising them because it will be impossible to recapture the moments of their youth.

If the foundation of your child/parent relationship is damaged due to abuse, neglect, regular negative criticism, and condemnation during childhood, it is likely your relationship as adults will be weak. It's possible that broken relationships between adult children and their parents can be restored, but it's usually very difficult. Rebellion and resentment in a household are often a result of parental hypocrisy. And these two monsters leave a bitter after-taste in one's heart.

"It is better to bind your children to you by a feeling of respect and by gentleness than by fear." — Terence (circa 185 – 159 BC)

One of the best ways you can improve your skills as a mother is by continually examining and assessing your own life. Be honest with your children and let them know that you don't get things right one hundred percent of the time. Remind your children that you are not perfect — and that you don't have to be, but continually strive to model whatever conduct you expect from them. However, don't make your shortcomings excuses for the wrong behavior. Show them how to use mistakes as springboards for positive change. Work to make sure that your encouragement and support tip the scale rather than your contempt.

When you work through issues yourself, you are able to coach your children through those same situations because you can relate to what they are dealing with; you are personally familiar with the tools they need to do it, too. How can you teach your child about overcoming trials and tribulations when *you* haven't done so?

Soul-searching is often a catalyst to making adjustments that will bring about positive changes in your family's life. There are numerous occasions in my life when I recognize and acknowledge that I am not doing what is best. During these moments, I fervently seek out God's help. What a blessing it is to accept God's grace and mercy to alter the course of our lives.

Finally, accept that in spite of all you do to be a positive example, your children will make their own decisions. You cannot live their lives for them. Your prayers, lectures and good role modeling will not prevent your children from making mistakes (just as you have). It is likely they will not do everything you expect and want.

You don't have to feel like a failure as a mother when you have done *what you were supposed to do and your children go astray*. **What you do to your children is between you and God; what your children do with their lives is between them** and God. No one can control human behavior except God. When your children choose a path contrary to what you taught and demonstrated, you must release them to God. Simply put: you cannot control every dimension of their lives. Therefore, continue to pray for God's mercy and grace to cover their lives.

"None of us can make our children godly...It's true that Proverbs 22:6 says 'train up a child in the way he should go, and when he is old he will not turn from it.' But that's not a guarantee—it's a principle. If you follow it, you give your children a wonderful foundation in life, but they will still make choices." (Rob Parsons)

Moreover, your children will need your guidance, grace, and patience when they fall short of God's expectations. **This is the time when you should demonstrate an example of unconditional love rather than judgment and condemnation.** These are the moments when your love must supersede your anger, frustration, and disappointment. (Read the chapter entitled, *Let Go and Let God*.)

Lastly, mothers must be an example of divine love. They must acknowledge and respect that their children are different from them. This is God's divine plan for humanity. No two human beings have the same fingerprint. God obviously intended for all of us to be unique. Your children have a remnant of you and a hint of their biological father, in addition to, a kiss of God's essence; this is what makes them who they are. Your total acceptance of your children teaches them how to love themselves and others. That's an example that can become a legacy for generations of your descendents.

"Charm is deceptive, and beauty is fleeting; but a woman who fears the LORD is to be praised. Give her the reward she has earned, and let her works bring her praise at the city gate." –Proverbs 31:30-31 (NIV)

Chapter Five
Take Care of Yourself

"If I could share one lesson from my battle with cancer, it would be this: We must free ourselves from the crushing and prolonged stress that can break down the immune system, leaving our bodies open to catastrophic illness. ...It is not enough just to change the way we treat our bodies; we must change the very patterns of our thoughts. We must empty ourselves of the resentment and bitterness that could poison our cells, and let love, faith compassion and forgiveness rule in their place." –Yvonne Williams, an ambassador for the American Cancer Society

Reflection Questions

1. What are you doing to take care of yourself (physically, emotionally, intellectually, and spiritually)?

2. Are you harboring any negative emotions (for your children's father, a family member, yourself...)?

3. What do you think would happen to your health if you never took a break from working?

Motherhood creates seismic changes in a woman's life. Mothers (single or married) are inundated with a myriad of complex job duties to fulfill. Not only is a mother responsible for providing her children's basic physical needs, she is also spiritually liable for loving, protecting and teaching them. This requires a level of personal accountability and selflessness that she might not anticipate.

From the second a woman becomes pregnant she has to think about how her decisions will affect her children. She can only give her children what she has; she can only teach them what she knows. **Although a mother doesn't single-handedly determine the final outcome of her children's lives, her thoughts, actions and words do shape their foundation.** The state of her children's lives is usually a reflection of the quality of her own life.

Therefore, it is imperative that a mother takes care of every aspect of her life. She must continually seek out ways to improve her well-being. No matter how busy a mother may be, her daily schedule must include an intentional action to respect her body, nurture her spirit and expand her mind with valuable knowledge.

"We mothers, whether biologically blessed with children or having children placed in our lives by other means, must remember that we can't afford to give ourselves totally away. Something must be left in reserve for the nurturer." (Serita Jakes)

You might be thinking: "If I take time away from work, I won't be able to meet my children's needs?" However, if you don't learn how to honor your health, you will be like a motor that overheats when it never stops running. A motor in a machine can be replaced, but you cannot ever be!

"A mother is one who can take the place of all others, but whose place no one else can take." (G. Mermillod)

There are three things I have learned to do that I believe contribute to wholeness and better overall health: releasing, reading and relaxing. **I believe these activities become powerful weapons for fighting the number one killer of single mothers — the failure to manage stress**.

Even if you only devote ten minutes to each of these three activities, you will significantly see changes in how you feel. Of course, always seek God for wisdom about every dimension of your life, especially your health. There are countless books on this topic, so you will never run out of resources to help you. It is extremely important though that you choose a regimen that best matches your personal needs.

Lesson One: Release

Every blue moon there is a news article that strikes a personal cord within me. Such was the case of a story about a man in a big city who killed himself by jumping off a seventh-floor balcony. Based on the information provided, the man was well-educated (he had a doctorate degree), respected in the community, married, and had children. He held a prominent position as a leader of a school that held a stellar reputation.

His story reminded me that no matter how much we achieve, one of our greatest accomplishments is attaining inner peace. What's happening inside of us can be a matter of life and death. Throughout the years, I have repeatedly taught my daughter that the most important value in life is not the acquisition of possessions, prestige, and power, but rather her life will only have purpose and meaning when she maintains a personal relationship with God, her Creator. This relationship leads us to the pinnacle of inner peace.

No human being is immune to adversity. Each of us will endure difficult moments in our lives. However, problems don't destroy us; it is our response to them that determines if we live as victims of unfortunate circumstances or if we celebrate victorious lifestyles. Our reaction to experiences is greatly influenced by our inner strength and attitude. These are not virtues we can put on plaques, educational degrees, and trophies; these are not tangible objects that we can purchase in a department store, yet they are the most powerful, life-sustaining forces we can possess.

As a mother, in order to stay healthy, you must learn how to constructively **release** negative energy which is rooted in your unmanaged human emotions, such as anger, jealousy and fear. This takes spiritual concentration and purposeful effort. For example, anger is a natural emotion, but if it isn't dealt with appropriately, it can become a lethal spiritual force in your life as well as your children's lives. On the other hand, when you (as a mother) work through emotional issues the right way, you create a positive model for your children to follow.

You cannot be an effective mother if you are not sane and whole. Even if it's not intentional, you will project your personal problems onto your precious children. This will affect how they see themselves and you as well as how they behave. Your children are observing everything you do and hear and internalize what you say; they need you to be in optimal health so you can be a source of love, sanity, strength, and wisdom. If you are suffering from **stress (something trying to run everyone scared stiff)**, your household will be chaotic and dysfunctional. The memories you create for your children will leave their ugly, indelible markings on their heart.

I am acquainted with a woman who almost allowed anger and resentment to cripple her as a mother. She couldn't fully enjoy the blessings God bestowed upon her because she spent so much of her time meditating on bad memories from her childhood. On the outside, (just as the man in the news article), she seemed to be doing fine. She was educated and had a decent job. She didn't carry herself like someone who needed to be committed to a mental health facility.

However, deep inside she harbored negative emotions about the abuse she had endured as a child. Although her mother had not failed to provide her with her basic needs, she repeatedly emotionally and verbally abused her. Her mother had even continued to have sexual intercourse for years with the very man who had sexually molested and harassed her. She felt this was the ultimate betrayal of a mother/daughter

33

bond. There were even times throughout her youth and adulthood when her mother demonstrated pure, unadulterated cruelty towards her and treated her as if she were worthless.

Rehashing these events during family visits always created more drama and the erosion of her mother/daughter relationship. No one ever acknowledged what had happened. In fact, she was expected to carry on a relationship with her mother as if it hadn't. Her mother had never offered a heartfelt apology. Instead her mother did the opposite: she justified the maltreatment of her daughter and labeled her as evil and rebellious, deserving of her abuse and much more. Consumed with grief, the woman didn't realize her mother's denial of her crimes against her was a typical human response to shame — a mechanism for self-preservation.

The woman had tried to release her pain by reflecting on the good moments she enjoyed with her family, but the truth was her painful experiences far outweighed the good ones. To make matters worse, she and her mother had rarely been able to share communication with mutual respect. So the woman didn't feel comfortable revealing her authentic self because each time she tried, she would be condemned criticized and judged by her mother who hadn't learned how to respect their differences.

One day as the woman expressed her anger aloud about the past a wise spiritual messenger interjected her lamentations and told her how bitter she sounded. The wise teacher reminded her that she could do nothing about the past, but needed to focus on the future relationship she had with her own child.

Her solution was to spend her time and energy trying to fix her own mistakes, problems, and faults. It was okay to acknowledge the past, but to blame her mother for all of her problems didn't make sense. The wise teacher's words held evocative power. From that moment, the woman began to divert her focus to her *own* responsibilities as a mother.

She began to release the malignant residue of her mother's toxic power over her and chose to focus on what she could control—her own life. She forgave her mother and reconciled that her past, even the painful moments, was ordained by God even if she didn't understand all the intricate details of why. She hadn't voted for her parents, but God had used His executive power to appoint them for a temporary term. Things had happened the way they were supposed to and she would no longer complain about the past.

"Forgiving does not erase the bitter past. A healed memory is not a deleted memory. Instead forgiving what we cannot forget, creates a new way to remember. We change the memory of our past into the hope of our future." (Lewis B. Smedes)

Complete release of toxic spiritual energy doesn't happen instantly. It begins and ends with daily, fervent and intimate communication with God. It takes time to let go of unpleasant memories. In order to heal your heart and mind, you must ask God to show you how to use your memories constructively.

You must accept that He has been in complete control of your life during both good and bad situations. Everything that has happened to you had a purpose. Let God teach you how to use your past to help others.

Some people will tell you to, "Just get over it!" If life were that simple the multi-billion dollar pharmaceutical companies would go out of business. Usually people who offer this prescription to problems either live in a state of denial or they haven't experienced what you have. There is no way they could fully understand your journey because they haven't walked in your shoes. Respect them, but connect with people who can coach you through your challenges because they know what you are feeling.

Memory is a God-given device that should be used to empower you to help others overcome what you already have. Only disease and death can destroy memory. Therefore, you must decide that when memories resurface, you will release the negative energy attached to them.

There is no need to relive disheartening experiences that you have already conquered. Those battles were won by God. In fact, they weren't really yours anyway. Use the lessons of your victories to defeat new foes – for there will be many. You are not merely a survivor, but you thrive today because of the love and mercy of a compassionate God.

"We all have our time machines. Some take us back, they're called memories and some take us forward, they are called dreams." (Jeremy Irons)

There are countless articles in medical journals and magazines about the mind-body connection. The emotions that dominate our lives have the potential to affect the equilibrium of our bodily functions, thus, creating disease and disorder. In other words, the better we feel emotionally, mentally and spiritually, the healthier we are physically.

Of course, there is so much we experience that is beyond our personal control. We cannot afford to meditate on that aspect of our lives. Worrying and talking about problems will not solve them; situations don't change as a result of thought. However, we can choose our attitudes. To release toxic spiritual energy, you must decide to let God deal with whatever you cannot. As Oliver Wendell Holmes once remarked, "the greatest act of faith is when man decides he is not God."

It took me a long time to understand that I could do nothing to preserve my life. I needed to stop worrying about everything that could go wrong. I tried to be a careful driver, but I still had a terrible car accident. I try to carefully manage my money and save, but unexpected expenditures always come up and deplete my bank account. I fiercely work to protect my daughter, but I cannot shield her from pain. Therefore, I resolved to be content (not complacent) regardless of what is happening in my life.

It sounds like it would be wonderful to be able to annihilate all of our problems, but most people would never celebrate how good God is if they hadn't experienced hard times. Actually, adversity catapults us into a life of activism, altruism and advocacy. We become models of triumph when we overcome misfortune and tragedy.

As single mothers, we often feel life is a target board and the world is incessantly throwing darts our way. We are constantly being told what our children cannot be and what they cannot have because their fathers are missing in action. Be encouraged with the knowledge that our spiritual enemy's fiery darts may hit its target, but will not penetrate to destroy us if we *release* what is harmful to us and our children to God.

Loving single mother, release your fears and worries right now. You are powerless to control all aspects of your life. God loves you and He will never forsake you. Release an unforgiving spirit! Release your anxiety! Release pain! Release ungodly pride! Release shame and guilt! Release evil thoughts! Release jealousy! Release greed! Release discontent! Release anger! Release low self-esteem! Release hatred! Release deceit! Release ungodly speech! Release everything that is an abomination to God!

"I waited patiently for the Lord; and he inclined unto me, and heard my cry. He brought me up also out of a horrible pit, out of the miry clay, and set my feet upon a rock, and established my goings. And he hath put a new song to my mouth, even praise unto our God: many shall see it, and fear, and shall trust in the Lord." (Psalm 40:1-3 KNV)

Lesson Two: Read

Reading is one of the most inexpensive (when using public libraries), therapeutic hobbies any mother can enjoy. In addition to the Holy Bible, wholesome magazines and books reveal information and perspectives that can enrich your life. God often speaks to us through a myriad of voices. Sometimes a character in a good novel helps you to reflect on your own life. Books often give you a chance to look at things from a distance instead of so closely that your vision is distorted.

Moreover, keeping abreast of the latest health news, historical and scientific discoveries, financial matters and ideas stimulates your intellect and allows you to make more informed decisions regarding you and your children. Not reading will create costly disadvantages. Ignorance is an expensive disease and reading is one of the ways you can cure it. Remember, you can only teach what you know. Without knowledge and awareness, you limit your possibilities for improving your family's state of being.

"To read is to fly: it is to soar to a point of vantage which gives a view over wide terrains of history, human variety, ideas, shared experience and the fruits of many inquiries." (Alberto Manguel)

God equips us with a brain and He expects us to use it. Intellectual health is just as important as good eating habits and exercise. There is an old saying: "If you don't use it, you lose it." Medical research has revealed that stimulating our brain keeps us youthful and mentally alert.

Regardless of how compact your schedule may appear, take time to read daily. Even if it's only for ten minutes, broaden your perspective on a plethora of subjects and share what you have learned with your children. As you acquire more wisdom and knowledge, you prepare yourself (and your children) for enriching opportunities.

Lesson Three: **Relax**

Having a job is needed to meet your family's financial obligations, but overworking can be detrimental to your health. Think about the old adage: Too much of a good thing can be bad. The key to being an effective mother is managing a life of balance and teaching your children how to do the same.

It's always good to work and play; laugh and cry; and pray and take action. For the rest of your life, you should honor yourself with moments of blissful relaxation. These moments allow you to refuel your spirit and energy to carry on your arduous duties as a single mother.

Throughout my life, I have heard of tragic stories of women suddenly dying of fatal heart attacks. One interesting factor about every case (stories in which I am personally familiar) is the woman died in her home, with the exception of one case in which she died in her driveway. I can't resist wondering if stress of overworking (inside and outside of the home) contributed to these mothers' untimely demise. I wonder if there a correlation with heart disease and the unmanaged stress women face due to all the duties they have as mothers. Why do so many women have heart attacks in their own home, a place which should be their refuge from stress?

"Sometimes the most important thing a whole day is the rest we take between two deep breathes, or the turning inwards in prayer for five minutes." (Etty Hillesum)

As I mentioned in a previous chapter, from the moment my daughter was born, a heightened level of anxiety invaded my spirit. I realized that I was not prepared for motherhood. I suddenly became cognizant of the awesome responsibility it takes to care for someone else, a fragile human being who would be completely dependent upon me. Unlike never before, I had an awareness of danger and despair in the world.

My tension was compounded with financial, personal and family problems. I soon learned that I needed to set aside some time to relax and manage my moods and emotional state. My daughter taught me that the mother/daughter spiritual connection activate their sensitive spiritual radars. They can sense something is wrong even when you're trying to hide it from them.

As a single mother without financial support and a stressful job, I learned to monitor my mood, attitude, and energy. I recognized that a mother affects the ambience of her home. If a mother is depressed, angry, fatigued, frightened, etc., her home will mirror her emotions. If she is constantly barking out directives and insults, she will create stress and chaos for her children. This is not an environment conducive to growing and learning.

"Most stress is optional." (Felicia C. Hardy)

Healthy mothers generate an atmosphere of positive energy, peace, respect, and love. This reduces the level of stress for herself and her children, subsequently resulting in a healthier family. The more a mother takes care of herself, the more equipped she is to support and nurture her children. She is the heart of her family.

Did you know that the human heart nourishes itself first, then the rest of the body? As a single mother, you are the heart of your family and you must nourish yourself first with fellowship with God, rest, knowledge and so much more. Just as the heart, when you have what you need, you can then pump what's essential to the rest of the members of your family.

You may feel if you take a break your household will fall apart. However, relaxing and giving yourself a moment to rejuvenate and refresh yourself will actually keep you going with a song in your heart. Relaxing means you have to interrupt your job duties with rest. Every day it's paramount that you enjoy a moment of inactivity. If you travail from dawn to dust how will you have energy and stamina to be strong?

You create a serious health risk when you never give your body and mind a chance to replenish what it continually expends. Rest does not necessarily equate sleep. When you rest, you might be conscious and alert, but exerting low amounts of energy. Keep in mind that rest isn't just a physical activity. You must also learn to rest mentally.

I know quite a few people who can't sleep at night because even though their bodies are run down with fatigue, they can't stop worrying about the cares of the world. Most of the time, they are suffering from discontent. There is something (or someone) they believe they need or want and they can't mentally rest because they don't have it. Instead of being grateful and making peace about what they already have, they are obsessed about what is absent in their lives.

If you're a mother who needs mental rest, I strongly encourage you to meditate on the following scripture: **"Not that I speak in respect of want: for I have learned, in whatever state I am, therewith to be content. I know both how to be abased and I know how to abound: everywhere and in all things I am instructed both to be full and to be hungry, both to abound and to suffer need. I can do all things through Christ which strengtheneth me."** (Philippians 4:11-13 KJV)

I also suggest creating a short list of personal affirmations about gratitude and contentment. It's good to set goals and strategize a plan to realize your dreams. Never allow yourself waddle in complacency. At the same time, don't devote useless mental energy to whatever or whoever is missing in your life. Only life-threatening issues deserve that kind of attention. You can live without the things you wish you had. If you believe you can, you will; if you believe you can't, you won't. Don't let your heart "arrest" you for putting undue stress on it.

Relaxation should take place when your surroundings are quiet. Maybe light some candles; deep breathe; and play soft music. During this time focus on yourself, personal aspirations, and your health. You can also do something you find enjoyable. I don't care how much work there is to do, learn to rest. As long as you are not in danger of getting a visit from the health department, delay completing some of your household chores for just a few moments. If you don't honor yourself, you will have nothing to give your beloved children.

Whenever you can, make relaxation a family affair. All homework and chores should cease for a certain period of time. Once you've given yourself a few moments to regroup and refuel your spirit, you can complete your daily duties and obligations less exhausted and overwhelmed.

When my daughter was growing up, as soon as we entered the house she had the habit of immediately starting her homework after a long day of school and extracurricular activities. Most parents would be proud, but I wanted to teach my daughter how to enjoy a balanced life. I taught her to take a break when she came home. I encouraged her to watch one of her favorite shows and/or get a snack.

Sometimes we would just have twenty minutes of complete silence, meditation, or deep breathing. Her homework always got done, but she was not stressed out. We didn't have a performance-based relationship. I encouraged her to do her personal best, but I was not obsessed with grades which can sometimes only be symbols of inert knowledge. Of course, I wanted my daughter to do well, but most importantly, I wanted her to "be well".

For the rest of your life, devote quality time to reading, relaxing and releasing. You will create a home where peace abides. You deserve some special time to nourish your mind, body and spirit. Honor yourself and your children with actions that will build their lives for service; activities that focus on what they can become, not merely what material things they can accumulate.

"I still need more healthy rest in order to work at my best. My health is the main capital I have and I want to administer it intelligently." (Ernest Hemingway)

Chapter Six
Building Healthy Relationships

"God calls us to individually and corporately represent Christ to the world, but our independence, pride and individualism often prevent us from becoming unified..." –Os Hillman

Reflection Questions

1. What quality of relationship do you have with your children?

2. Do your children see you as a loving and supporting mother or do they consider you abusive or neglectful?

3. What intentional actions have you taken to build healthy relationships with your children?

Like most things in life, good relationships between mothers and their children do not happen automatically or spontaneously. Righteous mothers understand that having a healthy relationship with each of their children is an essential aspect of good parenting that starts at birth. They recognize that being a tyrant and/or a dictator sabotages the possibility of having good relationships.

Therefore, they willingly give **all** of their children the same love, respect, and dignity that they want for themselves. They do not misuse their title and position to manipulate their children into doing solely what they want, but rather the will of God. They understand that their children are blessings (not burdens) from Him to be appreciated and loved.

As mothers, they recognize that they are merely stewards of God's property. They know that He holds them accountable for everything they think, say and do to *His* children. He has charged them with doing what is right and they take this responsibility seriously. In fact, righteous mothers believe that everything they do could be a matter of life or death to their children.

Motherhood to righteous women is about pleasing God and making sure their children are equipped with the tools to do His will. Their relationship with their children is a reflection of their intimacy with God. A good relationship with their children is a direct result of following His guidance and wisdom.

Generally speaking, children naturally yearn for a close relationship with their mothers. Even though the umbilical cord is cut at birth, a spiritual bond between mother and child remains for a lifetime. **This connection is strengthened when children feel loved, valued, and supported by their mothers.** However, it is weakened, and in some cases diminished, when mothers devalue, maliciously hurt, and neglect their children.

"Life affords not greater responsibility, no greater privilege, than the raising of the next generation."–C Everett Koop

Unfortunately, tens of thousands of people have strained relationships with their mothers. While this happens for a myriad of reasons, the most common is a result of abuse, neglect, and hypocrisy in a household. While people might honor and revere the title of mother, they often find it difficult to work through unresolved issues from childhood. The possibility of mending broken relationships seems like a dream that will never come true especially when mothers deny, trivialize, or even justify harming their children.

No one wants to become someone's punching bag or dart board, especially his or her mother's. I cannot count how many people I know (both young and old) who respect and love the women who gave birth to them, but choose to keep them in the balcony of their lives instead of the front row.

For most people, this decision is not about anger or resentment, it's about self-preservation. They cannot afford to add more stress to their already hectic lives. As children, they couldn't pack up and walk out of their toxic environments, but the second they became adults they ran as far away as they could from places that were littered with maltreatment, violence and hypocrisy.

Fortunately, this doesn't have to happen. It starts with a mother making the decision to have a good relationship with her children by any means necessary. She must be willing to teach her children good strategies for co-existing with people through modeling these actions herself. In other words, she must practice what she preaches. She must demonstrate all of the characteristics of wholesome relationships in every dimension of her own life.

Of course, healthy relationships are not one-sided. People must work together, but children will not know how to do this unless they are taught because they don't gain knowledge spontaneously. A mother is her children's first and most influential teacher. Through her words and actions, she must *show* her children how to: (1) communicate with love and respect, (2) listen, (3) demonstrate honesty, (4) forgive and (5) compromise. When children learn these essential skills at home, they are able to employ them in other relationships. The same is true for the opposite. If they never learn how to get along with the people at home, it will become difficult to have good relationships with people at school, work, etc.

I feel very blessed that my daughter and I are very close. In fact, it astonishes most people when they witness our special bond. This did not happen by accident. Our relationship is a result of me loving my daughter as I do myself. Since she was born, I have given her the same forgiveness, patience, support and so much more that I also want and need. In other words, I treated her as a human being, not as an animal or inanimate object.

Although my daughter and I spend a lot of time together, we don't consider ourselves friends. I will always be her mother and she will always be my daughter. Some things that she would do with an associate or friend, she might not ever do with me. We have mutual respect for each other. She reveres my title in her life but I continually taught her that positions of authority don't give people the right to be disrespectful and unkind, especially mothers.

In fact, as a mother I believe that I have an obligation to set a righteous example for my daughter. My faith in God leads me to understand that my daughter is not only an extension of myself, but she is a reflection of Him, her Creator. I sincerely believe that whatever we do to people, we do to God. If I mistreat my daughter, I am sinning against Him. Therefore, all of us should strive to give the best of ourselves to every person we know. We should honor people as priceless masterpieces designed by God.

Mothers must keep this in their heart while they are raising their children. Their precious babes will become adults faster than they think. It is imperative that mothers establish a healthy relationship with children from birth. When children can have a safe and nurturing relationship with their mother, they are less likely to desperately search for one outside of the home.

Mothers have a limited amount of time to set a strong foundation of character in their lives — to teach their children how to talk to people; how to actively listen; how to serve others; and be selfless. Whether mothers like it or not, they will model most of the things their children do. It would be wise that they make every moment count and use their time to demonstrate how to have good relationships.

Wonderful woman of God, you will always be your children's mother but your role will change as your children transition into adulthood. You can't ever recapture the moments of your children's youth. Do everything you can to create as many beautiful memories as you possibly can. These will sustain them through difficult times when you are no longer around.

Children will learn about life from you or someone else. They want to know that *you* can relate to the challenges they face. Sharing the lessons that you have learned along life's journey will strengthen your rapport with them. Children don't need you to be a Martian; they need you to reveal your humanity. They need you to "relate" to them by being transparent and honest. They also need you to be forgiving. Don't be afraid to let them know that you are not perfect and the forgiveness God has given you is what you will give to them.

On the next few pages, I will briefly discuss five of the most important characteristics of good relationships, particularly as it relates to motherhood. It would behoove you to seek out additional information about this very important aspect of motherhood. Above all, go to God who has all the answers you need to be a mother your children will cherish. He will speak to your heart. Let Him guide your thoughts, words, and deeds. Your relationship with your children will always mirror the relationship that you have with God. As you nurture and strengthen the bond you have with Him, you can build better relationships with your children.

"Call to Me, and I will answer you, and show you great and mighty things, which you do not know." – Jeremiah 33:3 (NKJV)

Lesson One: Communicate with love and respect.

I am acquainted with a woman who grew up in a place where ninety percent of her mother's communication was screaming directives, calling names, destructively criticizing her and communicating curses of failure and tragedy over her life. (Sadly, the mother continued to slander and criticize her daughter as an adult.)

At the age of eighteen on the very same day as her high school graduation, the woman left her mother's residence. Strangely, her mother seemed perplexed about why her daughter never wanted to visit her or why she rarely called. She never acknowledged her actions and in fact, she accused the daughter of being disrespectful for not taking the abuse — for not letting her "be a mother". Despite this woman's ugly childhood, the God in her wouldn't let her succumb to hate. However, the woman believed that God didn't create her for abuse and slander. While she loves, and honors her mother, she will never willingly subject herself to maltreatment and insults.

This story illustrates the damage that mothers cause in relationships when they fail to communicate with love and respect. Verbal abuse and negative criticism usually minimize the chances of having good relationships with children. Words are just as injurious or deadly as guns and knives. They can kill and destroy a person's spirit, sense of self-worth and faith. At some point in a person's life, he or she reaches the maximum tolerance level for toxic relationships. Sane and healthy-minded people will not accept abuse unchecked. They will stay away from mean people.

Therefore, a mother must communicate with her children in the exact same way she would demand for herself. I don't know too many people who enjoy being cursed out. Therefore, it's almost incomprehensible that a woman would do so to her own children. It is highly unlikely that she would accept that kind of language from a co-worker, family member or even a stranger. Just as her children, she wouldn't easily forget the painful feelings the hateful words caused.

Positive language builds good relationships while negative language destroys them. While people can forgive, and move forward, memories of the verbal abuse will always linger. Of course, God can heal our memories, but they can only be erased through disease and death. The damage is very hard to repair so to avoid this situation mothers must be extremely mindful of what they say to their children.

"The tongue has the power of life and death, and those who love it will eat its fruit." –Proverbs 18:21 (NIV)

Lesson Two: Listen

Listening is one of the greatest acts of humility and selflessness. Simply put, people cannot have relationships with people who refuse to listen to them. Again, being a selfish tyrant or dictator is an ineffective way to parent. Keep in mind that children need to talk. If they cannot talk to their mothers, they will seek out someone else with whom to do this important activity.

How could we ever have intimacy with people if we never allowed them to express their feelings, reveal their dreams, and lament their fears or problems? Listening is the quickest and most efficient way to find out what's happening in your children's life, not just physically, but what emotional and spiritual challenges they are facing.

If you never permit your children to use their voice and muzzle their speech, you will stifle their personal development and negatively impact their sense of self-worth. God gave us two ears for a reason. He wants us to listen twice as much as we speak. Again, He wants us to do unto others as He does to us. He listens to us and desires that we do the same to others, especially our children.

Whenever children communicate their feelings, do your best not to criticize them and put them down. However, with love, help them sort out and discern the things that are real from those that are illusions created by their imagination. **Use what you hear to guide your prayers. Refrain (and I know it can be hard) from focusing on problems. Emphasize the bank of solutions accessible to them. Guide them in discovering their potential to recover from mistakes.**

Whatever children discuss with you is confidential. No one but God should know what they have shared with you. They must believe that communicating with you is safe. Also, your reaction to their words will determine if they continue to come to you, their mother, the trusted confidant and sage. However, if you become bombastic and negative based on what you hear, you might miss an opportunity to teach your children grace and forgiveness and so much more.

As you listen, remember yourself. It's possible that your children are facing the same challenges that you already have. Think about how you would need someone to respond to you. Give those same allowances to your children. Share the wisdom you learned as you triumphed over your trouble. Always listen with compassion and love. In fact, articulate those things to your children no matter what they tell you. Your children will feel good coming to you about everything, instead of people who don't love them and might not guide them in the right direction.

"The law of the wise is a fountain of life, to turn away from the snares of death." –Proverbs 13:14 (NKJV)

Lesson Three: Demonstrate Honesty

As an educator, I have seen too many young people suffer because they followed bad examples. Children have a difficult time being able to cognitively understand consequences. This is why God doesn't beam them from the sky. He mandates that children be trained (raised) by their parents to live righteously. They need good mothers to teach them to be honest and do what is right, even under pressure. This is one of those critical lessons that children must **see.**

A mother's relationship with her children will be damaged if she *tells* her children to do right, but she *does* the opposite. The blatant hypocrisy will create rebellion in the home. Children will find it hard to respect mothers who unashamedly do wickedness in front of them and others, especially if their actions involve abuse or neglect. It will be hard to have a close and wholesome relationship with a mother whose actions bring shame to her family.

"The wise woman builds her house, but the foolish pulls it down with her hands." –Proverbs 14:1 (NKJV)

Lesson Four: Forgive

Forgiveness is essential for building and healing relationships. People make mistakes and forgiving them is one way of being an instrument of God's grace and compassion. God promises that if we forgive others, He will forgive us. As His true vessels, we should desire to forgive. We must remain respectful and loving to our children even when they disappoint us. After all, we are imperfect and have made countless mistakes, too.

It is unreasonable to be hostile or adversarial to our children when they fall because this is a critical time when they need our support the most. Children should believe that they can correct wrongdoing and triumph over problems just as we have. Forgiveness empowers them to look forward to a brighter future.

"Forgiving does not erase the bitter past. A healed memory is not a deleted memory. Instead, forgiving what we cannot forget creates a new way to remember. We change the memory of our past into a hope for our future." –Lewis B. Smedes.

52

The benefits of forgiveness far outweigh its opposite. First, we get closer to God. The more we seek Him out for comfort, the more of it we will have. He draws closer to us as we draw closer to Him. He helps us better understand ourselves and others. With His divine intervention, we learn how to use our energy and memory to focus on good things rather than the negative. This is what enables us to become stronger, healthier in every way, wiser, more peaceful, and more loving.

It's impossible to be whole without forgiveness. The weight of un-forgiveness wears us down and burdens us with darkness, mainly inwardly. This hinders the development of healthy relationships with others.

Loving Mother, demonstrate righteous character to your children by forgiving them as you want to be forgiven. Use their mistakes as teaching tools. Emphasize that recovery and transformation are always possible when we walk with God.

Lesson Five: Compromise

Selfishness is the enemy of love; it's the root of most problems in relationships. People cannot have unity and harmony with others when there is a lack of respect for their needs and desires. While children need to learn rules and boundaries that will save them from unnecessary suffering in relationships, they must also be given a chance to learn how to make decisions *with* others. **Teaching children that life isn't about having what they want all the time will prepare them for both service and leadership in the future.**

Healthy relationships are about working together and cooperation. However, everyone isn't going to be able to have his or her way one hundred percent of the time. **Compromise works as an adhesive to keep people together even when** differences exist among them. While there will always be non-negotiables created by the parent for the good of the family, compromise ensures that everyone gets a slice of the pie; no one gets a whole one. When mothers intentionally teach the value of alliance among their children, they will reduce issues of sibling rivalry and the psychological damage that favoritism causes.

When my daughter was a child I would teach her that she could get some of what she wanted, not all of what she wanted. We still use this definition of compromise today. Sometimes shopping would become interesting as she picked out her own clothing from a very early age. I would often repeat, "Remember the rule: you can get some items you want, but not everything." This lesson was just a tiny stepping stone towards knowing how to be a leader and how to make good decisions for herself.

While children need to be coached through the early stages of decision-making and compromise, they are likely to become good examples of team-players in the future. When children never learn how to negotiate and compromise at home, they find it difficult to do so in their adult life. They never learn how to subordinate their ego and work cooperatively with others at school, work, and home. Moreover, I have seen children "go wild" once they leave home and think that they are free from what they perceive as prisons instead of homes.

The bottom line is that mothers who straightjacket their children and never teach them how to compromise and work with others, inhibit them from learning how to be leaders and take personal responsibility. One of the most important goals of mothers is teaching their children how to stand on their own two feet. The home should be practice for the real world. At some point, they must leave the nest and fulfill God's purpose. Making sure that children are well-prepared for adulthood will reduce or eliminate their chances of having to repair their lives from poor choices.

Finally, having good relationships is an important aspect of life. Modeling how people should interact with each other is an invaluable lesson that will create immeasurable advantages for your children. Remember, the ways in which you engage with your children is how they will operate in relationships with other people (until they learn another way of doing things). Make sure you teach them how to **communicate with ALL people with love and respect.** Emphasize the importance of humbling themselves to patiently **listen to people without judgment or condemnation.** Demonstrate with your own actions as a mother **how to use forgiveness, compromise, and honesty** to build strong, long-lasting relationships. Never forget that as a mother, you are your children's first and most influential teacher. Your children are extensions of you. Always treat them the way you want to be treated. Most importantly, see them as God does—blessings to you and His world!

**"As far as possible without surrender, be on good terms with all persons. Speak your truth quietly and clearly, and listen to others, even the dull and ignorant; they too have their story. Be yourself. Especially do not feign affection. Neither be cynical about love – for in the face of all aridity and disenchantment is it perennial as the grass."
–Max Ehrmann (1872 -1945)**

Chapter Seven
Communicate Blessings, not Curses

"Whoever guards his mouth and tongue keeps his soul from troubles." –Proverbs 21:23 (NKJV)

Reflection Questions

1. What do you regularly say to your children?

2. Are your words usually positive or negative?

3. Do you use words to help or for punishment?

The words that mothers whisper or shout to their children remain with them forever. A mother's voice is usually the first and most influential her children will ever hear. **God intended for a mother's words to be teaching tools, not destructive weapons. He expects mothers to verbally articulate love, not hatred; hope, not hopelessness; potential, not problems; success, not failure; faith, not fear; and blessings, not curses.**

Mothers will be held accountable for every word they utter to their children. Maliciously assaulting a child with words has serious spiritual consequences. The words used to attempt to intentionally hurt a child will only destroy the mother. While God will cancel the curses of a wicked mother, the damage to her children will take time and great effort to repair.

I hate to sound redundant, but I must reiterate that mothers cannot be effective, loving, and supportive without a relationship with God. They will not understand the power and rewards of blessing their children when they are disconnected to Him. Again, having a strong connection with

Our Creator enables us to righteously fulfill our motherly duties, and communicate with love and respect.

It is our spiritual enemy who wants to kill, steal and destroy our children, and too often mothers separated from God become his artillery. On the contrary, God wants children to experience an abundant life. Children are reflections of His goodness. A mother's language and tone should be like a soothing balm, not an atomic bomb. The words that leave her mouth should represent God and His countless blessings for her children.

"But whoso shall offend one of these little ones which believe in me, it were better for him that a millstone were hanged about his neck, and that he drowned in the depth of the sea." –Matthew 18:6 (KJV)

Merriam Webster's online dictionary (2013) defines the verb, to bless, in several ways. The following are a few definitions: (a) to invoke divine care for; (b) to speak well of; (c) to confer happiness or prosperity upon; (d) to protect; (e) to preserve; (f) to endow; and (g) to favor. These definitions can help mothers to understand what words they should say to their children.

When a mother prays she should ask the Heavenly Father to make the words of her mouth and the mediation of her heart are pleasing to Him. (Psalm 19:14) Remember, as I said previously, when we sin against our children, we are actually transgressing against God. When we strive to please Him, we are empowered to daily profess protection, joy, and favor upon our children.

At times, the world can be a cruel and sordid place, especially for young people. Many children have to deal with bullying and conflict outside of the home. Children should find refuge in their mother's heart. A mother's voice should be stronger and more loving than all others.

If a mother repeatedly calls her children derogatory names, puts them down and condemns them for their mistakes and imperfections, it is likely that she will create a myriad of problems for her children. However, addressing problems without negative drama is a much better way for inspiring positive behavior.

God will help a mother be a blessing to her children by putting *His* words in her mouth. These words should articulate the blueprint for beautiful plans and purpose that God has designed for her children. Since blessings are ageless, she can bestow them upon her children if they are young or old.

It is inevitable that children will make tons of mistakes. A mother's response to any situation will have a direct impact on outcomes. Her words can lead to positive transformation and restoration or they can cause her children to feel disempowered which only leads to more problems.

Instead of screaming and insulting her children about their failures, she must speak the desired outcomes into existence regardless of how bad things appear in the natural realm. A mother's words are so powerful that they can reverse negative outcomes and rebuke the enemy of her children.

In other words, mothers must boldly profess that their children will be successful; they will overcome obstacles; and they will be triumphant; they will rise from a fall and be victorious in the end. The blessings she confesses and affirms with her mouth will be manifested through the supernatural power of the Holy Spirit that rules her heart. Her children will become what she believes and says that they will. This is the unlimited power of a mother's blessing.

"Now faith is the substance of things hoped for, the evidence of things not seen. For by it the elders obtained a good testimony." –Hebrews 11:1-2 (NKJV)

Chapter Eight
Emphasize Potential, not Problems

"My job is to take care of the possible and trust God with the impossible." (Ruth Bell Graham)

Reflection Questions

1. Do you emphasize your children's limitations or do you work to help them fulfill their potential?

2. Do you nurture their strengths or do you condemn them for their weaknesses?

3. What are you doing to develop your children's potential?

    I believe that God equips each of us with the confidence and ability to do great things before we are even conceived by our parents. Before we are manifested on Earth, we are made in Heaven by Him. Before the world began, we rested in God's womb. God cradled us in His bosom until we were released to our parents.

    From the moment we are born, it is our parents' responsibility to help us understand and fulfill our God-created potential. As I have said a thousand times, children should not be left to raise themselves. They need good parental support and guidance in order to become and remain whole, sane and productive adults.

    As children grow and develop, they should blossom just as beautiful flowers. Their first teachers and caretakers should feed them a daily diet of love, wisdom, and patience, etc. which act as the fertilizer, water, and sunshine to keep them physically, emotionally, spiritually and mentally strong and healthy.

While each of us has limitations, the focus should be on what we *can* do rather than what we cannot. We should be taught that limitations have a purpose, too. They remind us of how urgent it is that we depend on God throughout our lives.

However, they should not be stumble blocks, but stepping stones for greater levels of inspiration, humility, and compassion. While our weaknesses make us *feel*, our potential gives us the tools to *act* — to do the will of God. God, in His infinite wisdom pre-ordained us to make this world better. This might be achieved in both big and/or small ways, but nevertheless every one of us is called to add value to His kingdom. It is such as blessing to realize that Our Creator has gifted every human being with the tools he or she needs to be successful: to start and finish the work He has assigned to us.

"A man's gift makes room for him, and brings him before great men." –Proverbs 18: 16 (NKJV)

As a parent, it is urgent that you help your children discover their innate gifts that are blessings from God. Deep within your children there are rich treasures. Your job, as God's steward, involves helping to excavate those personal jewels. You can only do this when you are connected with the Creator. He must be your guide and source of wisdom. It is His providence that allows you to see and nurture the potential buried deep within your children.

The good news is that God didn't leave out a single child. Even if your child suffers from a disease or disorder, there is something special he or she can do to brighten this world. In fact, your child as a chosen vessel of God is to be the light and salt of this earth. Our children's light can illuminate an environment when they believe in themselves. Therefore, parents must instill a strong sense of self-worth and potential. Moreover, parents must emphasize that our value is not determined by the world, but God who created us.

Over the years, I have been blessed to see children rise above an infirmity and achieve their goals. In fact, just recently at my daughter's college graduation, I saw a young woman physically bound to a wheelchair get her college degree. With so many able-bodied young people dropping out of school, I couldn't help but note how significant and inspiring this accomplishment really was.

Helping our children reach their potential doesn't involve lying to them. If a child is blind, he probably won't become a pilot; if a child is paralyzed he or she will not be able to run in the Olympics. However, the goal of a mother is to focus on what the child *is capable* of doing. Furthermore, she must communicate this potential regularly with love and patience.

Children must know that even though they cannot do everything they want, they can still be SUCCESSFUL through the development of divine gifts. For example, a blind child might not be able to become a pilot, but he can certainly become an inspirational writer, musician, or teacher. And, even though a child who cannot walk will not be able to run in the Olympics, he or she can become a doctor, president of a company or screenwriter. In other words, our problems don't inhibit us from making contributions to the world. We are not completely impotent because one dimension of our lives is not perfect.

When you recognize your children's gifts, believe that God will open doors for those gifts to be nurtured. He will provide you with the support and resources to complete the task that He has given you as mother. He will never leave you or forsake you. If you trust Him, He will do amazing things in your children's lives. I can testify that God will outdo the best of biological fathers. He **"is able to do exceedingly abundantly all that we ask or think, according to the power that works in us..."** –Ephesians 3:20-21 (NKJV)

The key to empowering your children is unlocking your own potential as a mother. Your children will believe what you do. When they are young, they trust what you tell them. If you tell your children they are worthless, they will believe it. On the other hand, if you tell them they can do great things, they will believe that too.

Your faith in God unlocks the power to defy odds and overcome problems. Therefore, nurture your faith and your potential and power will get stronger. This allows you to aid your children with overcoming what you have already conquered yourself.

Finally, it is important to note that while each of us has the potential to do much good, we also have the capability of doing evil. I once heard a minister say that a parent never has to teach a child how to do wrong because he already knows. The aim of every parent should be teaching children how (and why) they can and must do what is right.

As I have mentioned throughout this book, children don't automatically have the knowledge they need to be successful. They don't have the cognitive ability to fully understand consequences. They need good spiritual coaches to help them navigate through multiple messages they are receiving each day. Only with the right kind of guidance can children discern what is helpful and what is harmful to them.

God mandates that caretakers and parents inculcate character as they raise their children. Again, teaching doesn't just involve telling. Moral instruction should always include modeling which begins with parents. Sometimes the best lessons are seen rather than heard. Hypocrisy is the root of anger, resentment, and rebellion in countless homes today. This can be avoided when parents *do* exactly what they want their children to do.

Additionally, when children miss a lesson, do not condemn them. Harassing them about their imperfections and mistakes will only make them feel inferior and inadequate.

Getting on the phone and humiliating your children by telling people about their mistakes will only exacerbate their problems. It will also seriously damage the possibility for having healthy relationships. Children must trust their mothers to help them instead of dehumanizing and shaming them.

Emphasizing potential to correct mistakes and resolve issues is an effective way of bringing out the best in children. Children respond well to positive affirmations, but are emotionally and psychologically damaged by put-downs and insults. Parents must be supportive of their children even when they fall. True love is not based on conditions. It is unwavering and isn't dependent upon circumstances. **While parents should not endorse wrongdoing, they can pardon their children and show them how to recover from fumbles and still make touchdowns in life.**

Most importantly, parents much teach children about the power of forgiveness by modeling it. Children must learn to forgive themselves and others in order to fulfill their potential. They must know that it's not how many times people fall, but how many times they recover and get back up that determines real character and strength. When children feel like hopeless failures and believe that they can never change, they will stop putting forth the effort to amend negative and destructive behavior. When parents, especially mothers, encourage their children, they will likely witness them triumph over their troubles. When the focus is on building potential, children have the power to rise above adversity and enjoy victorious lives.

"...whatever is pure, whatever is lovely, whatever is admirable—if anything is excellent or praiseworthy—think about such things." –Philippians 4:8a (NIV)

Chapter Nine
Discipline with Love

"Childhood does not determine an individual's destiny. However, it lays a foundation for every aspect of a person's life." –James Robinson

Reflection Questions

1. Are you treating your children the way you would want to be treated?
2. Are your discipline methods creating positive or negative behavior?
3. Are you punishing your children for being less than perfect?
4. Are your parenting techniques based on fear and intimidation or respect and love?

If children didn't need mothers to love, protect, discipline and teach them, they would be beamed from the sky like aliens featured in a science fiction movie. Certainly, this is not how humans are born. Furthermore, a child should not be expected to *train himself* how to "survive". Many of the important lessons children need to know aren't just learned automatically, they need to be taught.

Just as all children need a biological mother and father to create them, they also need parents to "raise" them. And, let me emphasize that children don't need any caliber of parents, they need **great** ones. Children especially need wise and wonderful mothers who instill godly values which enable them to appropriately take care of themselves and others.

Becoming a mother your children will respect, cherish and appreciate is not a result of wishful thinking; good parenting does not come automatically and doing what "you think is natural." (Unfortunately, some people believe abuse is a *natural* technique for parenting.) On the contrary, good parenting is a result of intentional efforts to do so.

Great mothers understand that the state of their own lives directly influences their children's well-being. The more they have for themselves, the more they can offer their children. Great mothers devote time and energy for improving their overall (mental, emotional, spiritual, and physical) health. This helps them to be blessings to their children.

Great mothers closely monitor their own behavior and continually make adjustments to do what is best for their children. This is not about mothers giving children what they want, but making sure they have their needs. They recognize that their children are totally dependent upon them until they can take care of themselves. They implement the best practices for parenting with patience and love.

Discipline is one of the most important, yet often stress-inducing aspects of parenting. As I mentioned in the introduction, there is simply no universal blueprint for producing healthy, law-abiding, productive, and God-fearing children. There is no one-size-fits-all formula for discipline. Every child is different and there is no handbook with custom-made instructions for each individual child.

"The formative period for building character for eternity is in the nursery. The mother is queen of that realm and sways a scepter more potent than that of kings or priests" (Author Unknown)

I have taught undisciplined, disrespectful children who come from strict religious homes. At the same time, I have dealt with exemplary students whose parents implement unorthodox styles of discipline. The bottom line is: in spite of what parents do, children will make their own decisions. It's an indisputable fact that parents cannot totally control their children's conduct. This is a natural dimension of their humanness.

However, mothers increase their chances of raising successful children when they establish and maintain safe and loving environments. Discipline that is implemented when children know their parents love them will eliminate rebellion and resentment in the home. The techniques we use to discipline our children will influence how they act, think, and speak. Moreover, discipline helps to shape their ideas about themselves in the context of their interaction with people outside of their families. Discipline builds character and character will have a profound effect on the overall quality of a person's adult life

"He who ignores discipline comes to poverty and shame, but whoever heeds correction is honored." –Proverbs 13:19 (NIV)

There are tons of studies by sociologists and psychologists that highlight the correlation between a childhood environment and adult behavior. For instance, the majority of criminals on death row grew up in homes dominated by violence as well as severe physical and/or sexual abuse. Of course, there are always exceptions to any rule because there is a complex matrix of variables that ultimately determine human behavior.

Throughout my career as an educator, I've witnessed the cycle of cause and effect operating in my students' lives. I began to notice that my good students, those who were respectful, studious and motivated, shared common habits that had been taught in their homes (many lead by single mothers). This helped me to reflect on how I was raising my daughter. I applied the lessons I learned to my own parenting style and I have decided to share some them with you in this book.

Of course, my daughter is not perfect. She has made many mistakes, but I see the evidence of good character, and most importantly, she acknowledges a personal relationship with God. We are close and communicate on a regular basis with mutual respect and honesty. I understand that she is, as I am, a work in progress. There is so much more for each of us to learn. Although my role in her life is slowly changing, I am still her personal, spiritual coach and most enthusiastic cheerleader.

As you read the following pages, keep in mind that the most valuable wisdom and insight should come directly from God. Your children were created by Him; He knows more about them than anyone else. Every day communicate with God on your children's behalf. Take actions based on God's wisdom. He has a fail-proof system of discipline that involves having love, patience, and forgiveness for your children. Doing things His way will result in your children becoming adults who revere God, His Earth, and His people.

Lesson One: Observe each child.

Children need attention. Ignoring them is a non-negotiable. Paying close attention to their behavior will help you discover what your children need. If you spend most of your time working or chasing a man, your children will feel they are missing an essential ingredient in their lives—you. They need a mother's unconditional love and affection.

Whatever you refuse to give them they will try to find in someone or something else. This person or thing may not be in the best interest of your child. Always use your observations to direct your prayers. Ultimately, your prayers should evoke positive actions to support each child becoming the best he or she can.

Lesson Two: Discover what each child needs.

Every child is different. Your actions cannot be generic when parenting. Giving a child what *you want* instead of what he or she needs can result in discipline problems. Determine what each child needs through observation, direct communication, and prayer. We have all heard stories about parents making an awful, surprise discovery about a child. This is less likely to happen when a mother is paying attention. Awareness involves both physical and spiritual sight. Pray that God opens your eyes so you can see and discover what your children need to be successful. I often wonder how a mother would not know her teenaged son can't read, hear, etc. Is it because she isn't paying attention to her child?

Lesson Three: Do what works.

There are people who say, "If you spare the rod, you will spoil the child." There are others who say corporal punishment is a form of abuse and causes a host of psychological and behavioral problems. As a mother, incorporate discipline that works. If corporal punishment isn't changing your child's behavior, why continue to use it? If talking and time-out aren't effective, why not try corporal punishment the right way? An important factor in effective discipline is balance. A good mother gives the right amount of everything at the right time. Would the right use of corporal punishment for a three year old produce the same response as it would for a fourteen-year-old? Again, I cannot emphasize enough how important it is to seek God for solutions. His answers hold the key to positively transforming your children's actions.

"The family was ordained by God that children might be trained up for Himself; it was the first form of the church on earth." (Pope Leo XIII)

Lesson Four: Communicate with respect.

Words can hurt. Be careful about the tone and choice of words you use when you talk to your children. If a mother repeatedly calls her children derogatory names, puts them down and condemns them for their mistakes and imperfections, it is likely that she will create a myriad of problems for her children. **When you employ negative communication with your children, you chip away their sense of belonging and self-worth. While people can heal from verbal abuse, the process of recovery is usually long and arduous.**

Mothers must learn to guard their emotions. If they cannot be positive, they should learn to remain silent. Addressing problems without drama is a more effective way for inspiring positive behavior. Children need mothers who emphasize solutions and potential, not problems. Using anecdotes, explanations, and examples instead of screaming at your children is a more effective way for improving behavior. This increases their comprehension of a lesson as well as encourages a relationship of mutual respect.

Lesson Five: Listen.

Some parents never allow their children to express themselves. They oppress their children's voices and muzzle their ideas and dreams. This is another contributor to discipline problems. Children who don't have an opportunity to express what they feel often suffer from inner turmoil. They fail to learn how to communicate with others which leads to problems in future relationships. Communication is the key to greater intimacy with your children. The closer you are to them, the better opportunity you have to help them.

Listening builds trust between you and your child. The more comfortable your children feel about confiding in you because you are a respectful listener, the more likely you will maintain a close relationship in the future.

Teach your children to communicate with respect by setting an example for how to do this. They were borne with a mouth for a reason. God wants them to use their voice for good and not for promoting evil. As a mother, make time each day to listen to your children. Your ears are a direct link to what is going on in their hearts and minds. **Don't judge and condemn them for their feelings. Your job as a mother is to help them work through issues. You can't do that if you won't even listen to them. As I have repeatedly said, you must give your children the same love, forgiveness, patience, etc. that you need and want for yourself.**

Lesson Six: Accept differences.

It may be shocking for some readers, but there are mothers who don't like some of their children. They can't get beyond a child's personality because it's different from their own. They try to re-design what God created instead of teaching character and letting their children be who they were called to be.

Personality is inherited (it's a combination of you, your child's biological father, and a touch of God); character is something you learn. It may be hard to accept but your children were made for God's purpose. He is the architect of their personality. How they were made will equip them to fulfill His purpose. Character is the key to protecting their purpose. Through character, they will keep what they earn and finish what they start. Since wisdom doesn't fall out of the sky, God uses people as His mouthpiece. You are your children's first and most influential teacher. Love them as they are. Accept that the differences among you and your children are God-ordained.

Lesson Seven: Create an environment conducive to learning and growing.

It's difficult for children to be healthy and happy when they are surrounded by chaos and confusion. The more peaceful your home, the fewer discipline problems your children will have. Their primary environment — your home, becomes a mirror of their conduct. If your home is noisy and dysfunctional, you must release the people and activities that are creating the negative energy. This could be a matter of life and death for your children. It is pure selfishness to not make adjustments in your household that benefit your children.

"Children will not remember you for the material things you provided but for the feeling that you cherished them." (Richard Evans)

Lesson Eight: Seek out support.

If you feel overwhelmed, seek out help. Look for other mothers who won't be judgmental because they have worn your shoes. There is no shame in admitting that you're having a difficult time. It is insanity to think your circumstances will magically or instantly change. There are countless nonprofit organizations that are willing to help you. Remember, everything you do is creating a memory for your children. Get help so they won't be haunted by the nightmare you created.

Lesson Nine: Don't defend children when they are wrong.

One of the worst things you can do is make excuses for your child's bad behavior and defend him when he is wrong. This will teach your child that he is above authority and laws, and that he can do whatever he wants. This contributes to his delinquency and he sees you as a human ambulance to rescue him when he gets into trouble. This will enable him to become disrespectful and selfish. What's worse is that you eventually become a casualty of his contrary spirit.

71

Lesson Ten: Monitor your response.

We are all born with the propensity to make mistakes and we will do so often. Children are not perfect and never will be. They need someone to teach them how to do what is right and work through their issues. When they fall short, use this time to teach them strategies to overcome a problem. Give positive feedback. Don't judge and condemn them for falling short. Give them the same mercy and grace that you want for yourself. How you respond to their mistakes will determine if things improve or if they get worse.

You can tell your children what they are doing wrong, but that doesn't give clear instructions on how to transform their behavior; pointing out flaws never changes people's conduct. You can tell a child he is disrespectful and rude, but how did that help? If you coach the child on how to reverse that conduct, using illustrations, you will get better results. Instead of fussing, say, "this is what you need to do when…" Explain the cycle of cause and effort. Help your child understand the purpose and benefits of doing what you're asking.

Learn to speak calmly. Model the behavior you expect from your child. Be patient. Be willing to teach a lesson multiple times. Children do not have the cognitive ability to understand complex concepts. You must repeatedly break things down for them. You must patiently teach and re-teach important lessons. Your reward for doing this is improved behavior.

Finally, never forget you made mistakes and will continue to do so. Demonstrate the same allowances, unconditional love for your child that you desire for yourself. Some people are selective about who they will forgive and tolerate. They will give their boyfriend or lover a million chances to correct his behavior, but they seem to have no patience for their children and/or other people. Situations like these produce rebellion and resentment. **"The future destiny of the child is always the work of the mother."** (Napoleon Bonaparte)

Lesson Eleven: Strive for balance.

Your children get tired too. School can be a very stressful place. Therefore, teach your children how to live balanced lives. (Read the chapter entitled, *Take Care of Yourself*). **Discipline problems can be worse when children are stressed out with school, chores, personal problems, etc. Your job is not to be a slave master and use your children for your personal gain. They need the right balance of work and play to be healthy and whole.** Teach your children that while hard work is important, taking time to relax is also essential for being happy and healthy.

Lesson Twelve: Teach.

Merely telling your children what to do is not an effective parenting technique. Additionally, doing things for your children that they can do for themselves is equally damaging. Teaching on the other hand has countless benefits. **"...I've always believed that children are little adults, and at the end of the day, you have to teach them how to be responsible for their own lives. As parents our job is to take their power and use it in a way that is pro-life, not take all of our child's power to make them do things we want them to do."** (Jada Pinkett-Smith)

Teaching, as mentioned previously, involves detailed explanations, illustrations, giving a purpose for an action, examples, and safe exposure to problems you want your children to avoid. For instance, show them examples of the effects of drug abuse. Also, expose them to people are successful and teach them the strategies these people used to realize their goals. Good teachers allow their students to ask questions and communicate their ideas. Again, your children are your students. You must teach godly principles, not just talk about them.

Finally, don't wait until a crisis surfaces to teach wisdom. The best lessons are taught during a time of peace—a time when things are going well. A soldier doesn't learn how to shoot a gun in the midst of a battle. He gets strenuous military training **prior** to combat.

Your children can't overcome obstacles unless you prepare them (in advance) to do so. The element of surprise is an effective tactic for destroying an enemy. Your children shouldn't be knocked down by shock. Equip them with the armor of godly wisdom to conquer their spiritual enemy. Teach and re-teach principles that will build their lives to do God's purpose. Your time for laying a foundation is limited.

"Tell a child what to think, and you make him a slave to your knowledge. Teach him how to think and you make all knowledge his slave." (Henry A. Taitt)

Lesson Thirteen: Make every moment count.

Your children will be adults faster than you think. You have a limited amount of time to set a strong foundation of character in their lives. Make every moment count. Spend the majority of your time with them doing positive things and creating good memories. You will always be your children's mother but your role will change as your children transition into adulthood. You can't ever recapture the moments of your children's youth.

Give your children the "wings" they need to fly from the nest and soar above obstacles and difficulty. The beautiful memories you create for them will become the wind they need to fly high during critical moments.

"Give a little love to a child and you get a great deal back." (John Ruskin)

74

Lesson Fourteen: Don't compare a child to anyone else.

No one is exactly like your child. You did not choose your children. God assigns children to the parents He wants them to have. Comparing a child to other people will negatively impact his/her self-image. Point out models of exemplary behavior, but focus on the strategies for success.

Don't punish your child for not meeting all of your expectations. Don't put them down for being less than perfect. Don't devalue them because you don't think they can bring you glory. Don't encourage them to become like someone else. Don't punish them because they remind you of their father — a man for whom you might harbor resentment. (Keep in mind your children didn't get all of their traits from their father. Your child's personality is a combination of *you*, the father and God. Please work to stop blaming a child's faults on his/her father.) Your overt hatred for your ex, especially when you compare your child to that person, can potentially create deep psychological problems.

When a child becomes obsessed with being like someone else, he neglects accepting and appreciating his authentic self. Moreover, when a child is compared to an unfavorable person his sense of self-worth and significance is distorted. Depression in a child is often the result of him not being comfortable with his own unique identity.

Lesson Fifteen: Share the lessons learned from your mistakes.

Children will learn about life from you or someone else. They want to know that *you* can relate to the challenges they face. Sharing the life lessons that you have learned along life's journey is a powerful tool to enhance discipline. Children don't need you to be a Martian; they need you to reveal your humanity. You are not perfect. Your struggles from yesterday are their struggles of today.

Let your children know that we all fall down, but we can get back up. Making mistakes is an integral aspect of life. Mistakes don't have to destroy us; the most important lesson they will ever learn is the process of correction and recovery. If they know that you were able to change and/or overcome obstacles, they will believe they can too. Yes, it takes courage to be transparent and reveal your failures, but the child/mother bond is strengthened when your children see you as an example of resilience and triumph.

"Don't let failure define you. Let it refine you. Learn to fail forward." (Valorie Burton)

Lesson Sixteen: Encourage each child to be his or her personal best.

When my daughter was growing up, I never encouraged her to compete with other children. I repeatedly coached her to do her personal best at all times. Competing with her own self was a better way to monitor and assess her progress. As an educator, I had seen so many examples of unhealthy competition. This resulted in me teaching my daughter that it is exhausting trying to outdo someone else. When you strive to be "the best", your focus is on performing *better than* someone. Therefore, when you're not number one you feel inferior and defeated.

I am grateful that my daughter embraced this idea. I believe it alleviated undue stress and peer pressure from her life because her focus was on herself rather than other people.

Inculcate in your children's heart that they are just as intelligent, beautiful, worthy, etc. as any other child. Encourage them to do their personal best and not waste energy and time trying to conquer the world. If their personal best leads them to the top, fine. If it doesn't, it's still fine. You will take so much pressure off your children when you teach them to do their best and let God deal with the rest.

Lesson Seventeen: Embrace change.

When many women get pregnant, they only prepare for bringing home a *baby*. Rarely do they consider having a toddler, a child, a teenager, a young adult and a woman or a man. Motherhood involves a series of continual changes for both you and your children. Some of the changes you might anticipate, but many of them you won't.

"Change has a considerable psychological impact on the human mind. To the fearful, it is threatening because it means that things may get worse. To the hopeful, it is encouraging because things may get better. To the confident it is inspiring because the challenge exists to make things better." (King Whitney, Jr.)

As your children's most influential teacher, you must help them understand the value and purpose of change. Great mothers have a deep connection to God. They know that change is one of His mechanisms for spiritual transformation and growth. Every experience we endure is a part of His divine plan. There are so many events that happen beyond our control. However, our trust in God remains unshaken knowing that all things work out in our favor and either we can cry about them all day or we can claim our hidden blessings. These changes are divinely made on our behalf.

Additionally, there are changes that we must orchestrate ourselves in order to operate as our personal best. God is not a gangster who hijacks our spirit to force us to embrace certain behaviors. He will help us, but we must invest the time and energy into positively transforming our lives. The biggest resistance surrounding this kind change is our tendency to do what is familiar or comfortable. The unknown conjures up so many of our fears and distortions.

I assure you as a fellow mother that your children will transform into beings that you will not readily recognize and accept at times. It would be foolish to expect our children to mentally remain the same throughout their lives. Great mothers are flexible and understand that they must change how they interact with their children as they grow up.

Lesson Eighteen: Have discussions.

When my daughter was growing up, my primary discipline tool was the art of discussion. (Yes, I did far more talking than I did spanking.) I spent a lot of my time talking to my daughter about a wide range of topics, even when she was just a toddler. I did my best to use age-appropriate language, but there were times when I couldn't avoid being straight-up and raw. More significantly, I allowed my daughter to ask questions, and I wasn't afraid to answer them.

Additionally, I used movies, books, events in the news and personal experiences as springboards for these discussions. I continually emphasized that there are two ways to learn something: You can touch the stove and get burned or you can watch someone else touch it. Listening and observation are two powerful learning tools to avoid unnecessary suffering.

As I raised my daughter, I wanted her to feel like she could talk to me about anything. I always permitted her to express her own ideas. Instead of telling her what to think, I helped her sort out the truth—how to distinguish the difference between fact and fiction.

Children should know the truth. They need wise teachers (mothers) to help them uncover and disclose what is real. This protects them from many of life's avoidable pitfalls. Misconstrued messages and illusions fabricated by entertainment wizards can confuse children. When they get a distorted sense of reality, they can't make good decisions. A mother must be willing to help her children discern what is true.

Some parents believe children shouldn't talk to adults. They silence their children and oppress their ideas. These children never learn how to articulate their feelings and become slaves to other people's thinking. They do poorly in classrooms that demand they critically think and explain concepts. If you keep your children silent, that's how they will remain when they are having problems. You will be the last to know what's happening to them and unfortunately, it may be too late to save them.

The human brain is stimulated by inquiry. Children are naturally inquisitive and like to explore things. They will bombard you with questions so you must be patient and prepared to answer them. They will ask you, "why", more times than you can count. You must be willing to discuss the answers. This creates a situation when children understand that doing what you ask is not only beneficial to the family, but to them personally. Just remember, if your brain is empty as a mother, you will have nothing to teach them. (Read the chapter entitled, Take Care of Yourself.)

"Tell a child what to think, and you make him a slave to your knowledge. Teach him how to think and you make all knowledge his slave." –Henry A. Taitt)

Lesson Nineteen: Monitor their friends.

I can't count how many children's lives I have witnessed either improve or get worse due to the company they kept. I taught my own child that people are like elevators: they will either take you up or they will take you down. When she was growing up, I closely monitored her friends. I would determine how much time, and in what settings, I would allow her to spend with various people.

There were certain people she could be closer to than others. It was important for her to know that she must love every human, and that she was not better than other people. However, it was important to avoid close relationships with people who practiced destructive lifestyles.

Some people could have VIP status in her life and sit on the front row while others would have to sit far in the balcony. I allowed her to communicate with people from all walks of life, and with varied backgrounds, but her close friends — the ones she could hang out with, were people of character.

Know with whom your child is interacting. Teach your children that through association they can reap benefits or they can reap untold pain. You will have fewer issues with discipline if your children befriend people who are involved in constructive and wholesome activities.

Lesson Twenty: Invest in extracurricular activities.

When children are involved with character-building activities like sports, girl scouts and boy scouts, music and dance, they are less likely to get entangled with negative activities. As a single mother, you might feel that limited finances will inhibit your children from participating in extracurricular activities.

I want to encourage you to nurture your faith and believe that God will make a way out of no way. To finance an extracurricular activity, seek out a sponsor in your family or community, cut back on items you don't need or find activities that are inexpensive.

I must admit that I was extremely blessed to have a supportive family who compensated for the monetary child support I needed. My daughter was financially blessed on her birthdays, holidays, and special occasions. This money was used to pay for the numerous activities in which she participated. These activities taught her about hard work;

collaboration and leadership; built confidence; and provided her the positive attention that all children need to feel confident.

To meet my financial needs, I believed through faith that God would bless me. God proved that He would not forsake the fatherless. I boldly proclaimed through faith, my daughter would not be paralyzed financially even though I was operating with one income. I will always believe that God has an unlimited supply of whatever resources I require. Whatever God did for me, He will also do for you. Believe and teach your children to have faith, also.

"Expect great things from God; attempt great things for God." (William Carey)

Lesson Twenty-one: Love your children unconditionally.

Children who know they are loved are generally better behaved than those who don't feel that way. Love is the most essential ingredient to feeling confident and valued. Love your children when they do good things; love them when they do bad things. Love your children when they make you proud; love them when they disappointment you. Love them when they succeed; love them when they fail. Tell your children you love them every chance you get. Let them know you must discipline them and teach them character because you love them.

When love is the guiding force for all of your actions as a mother, you will significantly reduce discipline problems in your home. Continually nurture your relationship with God, the ultimate source of love. You will create a priceless legacy that future generations of children will honor.

"[Your] children will not remember you for the material thing you provided but for the feeling that you cherished them." –Richard L. Evans

Finally, good discipline is what prevents human disaster. Your children need (and actually desire) constructive discipline. Keep in mind that negative techniques for dealing with behavior will usually lead to unfavorable results. The strategies in this chapter work. As an educator for over twenty years, I have seen the very best and worst of behavior. Parents who are pro-active and see problems as teachable moments have better outcomes than those who are reactionary and explosive.

Children need adults who can assist them with working through their problems with love and patience. **Condemnation, criticism, and violence do not work. They are ineffective ways for improving behavior.** These destructive forms of discipline hinder children rather than help them. Measure the effectiveness of your discipline techniques by what you observe. Do you see improvement or is the situation getting worse? Remember, it makes no sense to do something that doesn't create favorable results.

As always, seek God's wisdom and power when choosing the best forms of discipline for your beloved children. He is the best Counselor for tailor-made techniques that will perfectly fit every child according to his or her needs. Keep in mind that when love permeates in a home, the less discipline problems will exist. God's unfailing love prevents resentment, anger, sibling rivalry, favoritism, un-forgiveness, hypocrisy, and discord. Therefore, let love be the first strategy for effective discipline. More love means less behavior issues.

Chapter Ten
One Day at a Time

"Mothers are really the true spiritual teachers."
--Oprah Winfrey

Reflection Questions

1. What do you worry about?

2. How has focusing on the future (or the past) benefited you and your children?

3. Can you control everything that happens in your life?

During my pregnancy, I recall spending a lot of my time reading about how to care for a baby. Most of the information I gained dealt with the physical care of a child. I wasn't exposed to knowledge about the life-altering emotional and mental adjustments that would involuntarily occur after giving birth.

Being suddenly and totally responsible for another person heightened my sense of human limitations and mortality. Knowing that my child would be totally dependent upon me for every aspect of her fragile life made me more aware of my imperfections, and feelings of inadequacy. For me, motherhood made me judge the world differently and my purpose within it.

Fear about my limitations gradually started to dissipate the more I believed that God's perfection would compensate for my weaknesses. I accepted that no matter how hard I tried, I would never be able to fully protect my child, but God was willing and able to do what I could not do with my finite human strength and power.

During my 23 years as a mother, I have learned that I have only two choices as a parent. I can worry all day about every abhorrent thing that could occur or I could embrace the peace that only God can give.

The more I take action to fortify my faith in God, the stronger and wiser I become. Throughout the years, I have learned a powerful lesson: God doesn't change life, but He changes people. Trusting Him will not exempt me from unpleasant and uncomfortable circumstances, but walking with God allows me to respond to life's challenges as a victorious woman rather than a perpetual victim.

It is not necessary for me to understand why things happen as they do. God is not less powerful or less loving because my life isn't perfect. However, I know without a granule of doubt that God always puts a powerful spiritual treasure hidden behind every trial. Yes, there are moments when I have cried myself to sleep in anguish, but God's presence through it all has kept me sane and hopeful. I now know that talking, reading and learning about God are totally different from actually walking with Him daily through the valleys of life. Yet, this is one of the only ways to fully experience the magnitude of His eternal love.

Taking one day at a time and not being anxious about your children's future is like most things: it's much easier said than done. However, worrying never changes outcomes; it never solves problems. The result of anxiety is dangerous stress and negative mental distortions. When we worry, our emotional and mental equilibrium begins to send distress signals throughout our bodies that can potentially cause disease and disorders.

As mothers, we must accept that not knowing the future is okay as long as we stay connected to God — the one holds the future. In order to be healthy for our children, we cannot inundate our minds with the cares and tribulation of this world. God's presence in every situation is sufficient. God has equipped us with the tools to endure whatever trouble comes our way. He will never put more on us than we can bear. He is faithful to remain with us through stormy days as well as those brightened by sunshine.

Therefore, we must let faith, not fear be our compass every single day. Each day that we feed our faith in God is each day that we starve our fear. Taking one day at a time becomes easier when we are walking with God. We must grip His hand and never let go. We must never try to do the work that only God can do. Surrendering and submitting to His will allow Him to do His job without interference. All we can do is let Him help us do ours. Simply put, we cannot take our next breath without Him and we need Him to sustain us each and every day.

"Therefore do not worry about tomorrow, for tomorrow will worry about its own things. Sufficient for the day is its own trouble." –Matthew 6:34 (NKJV)

Chapter Eleven
Life without A Man

"No man is worth your tears, but once you find one that is, he won't make you cry." (Author Unknown)

Reflection Questions

1. Are you obsessed with finding a man to help you?

2. Do you think your children are less fortunate because their father is "missing in action"?

3. Are you harboring negative emotions about your children's father? If so, are these emotions affecting how you see and/or treat his children?

4. Have you asked God to help you get through a season of celibacy?

5. What kind of men do you have around your children?

6. How are your relationships with men affecting your interaction with your children?

7. Have your children seen a series of men come in and out of your life? If so, have you considered how this is psychologically affecting them?

Although our world is blessed with honorable men, many women are forced to raise children alone due to divorce, irresponsibility and even death. There is also a group of women who are married, but technically classified as single mothers because despite their marital status, they are solely responsible for raising their children.

Whenever men abdicate their responsibilities as fathers, women have no choice but to take on the job duties of two parents. Of course, it is not easy, but God has a way of compensating for whatever we are lacking in our lives. However, for most mothers, it is their greatest hope that their children interact with a loving father who would not hurt them.

Although I do not believe that single parenting was our Creator's original blueprint for the family, our effectiveness as mothers is not diminished because of the absence of a father. If a man chooses to abdicate his obligations to his children, we as mothers must make one of two choices: (1) we will move on with our lives and choose to become wiser and stronger because of our experiences, or (2) we will meditate on our losses and spend all of our time and energy grieving about what is missing in our lives.

I, too, like most women, fantasized about having the ideal family. This included getting and staying married to one man as well as having children. I dreamed of having a beautiful home surrounded by a picket, white fence and family vacations across the country and abroad, but because of my ignorance and poor choices, my life had a different outcome.

For a while, I internalized all the negative statistics concerning single-parent homes even though there were thousands of success stories of fatherless children—children who grew up to become examples of resilience and hope like Judge Sonia Sotomayor, pediatric neurosurgeon, Dr. Benjamin Carson, and actor, Denzel Washington. All three were raised by single mothers, yet they rose above their disadvantages. In fact, I knew from my experiences as an educator that a two-parent home was no guarantee that children would turn out any better than those with one parent.

When my daughter was around six years old I got married because I wrongly thought her life would be better with a father in the home. One of the many lessons I learned from my gross mistake was that children don't need a father, they need a GOOD father. Having an unrighteous man around them would actually be detrimental to their welfare.

Additionally, allowing children to live in an environment of hostility and chaos with two parents would be far more damaging than living in a more tranquil home with one peaceful and sane parent. I cannot emphasize that peace is truly priceless, particularly for children. Unfortunately, some people won't ever value peace until they've experienced a nauseating amount of its opposite. There are also people addicted to drama. They can't feel comfortable in a peaceful environment, so they purposely create chaos and turmoil.

Eventually at some point, I resolved to give up trying to *find a man to rescue me* and turned to God for all of my needs. I decided to embrace a season of solitude; I promised God that I would accept a life of celibacy and I would not date, at least until my daughter graduated from high school.

Some people thought I was crazy, and felt that for a young woman to pledge to be single for an extended period of time was an unfair, self-imposed sacrifice to make, even for a child. However, giving myself some time to sort through my emotional baggage, let God heal my broken spirit and make personal adjustments, actually contributed to me becoming a more effective mother and more confident woman.

Furthermore, I did not believe that having men in and out of my life was a wholesome example of womanhood for my daughter. Of course, it would be nice to be *happily* married, but there has never been a day that I regretted my decision to take a hiatus from being in a relationship. In fact, I can't thank God enough for giving me the wisdom and strength to do it.

During this phase of my life, I taught my daughter that with God's help she could have just as much (and more) as any other child. As long as we stayed close to God, there would be no limitations to what she could achieve. No human, not even me, determined the final outcome of her life.

She belonged to God and she should spend the rest of her life nurturing an intimate relationship with Him. I coached her almost every day on ways she could build good character and enjoy a productive life. I didn't make her feel that she couldn't have certain things because her father wasn't around. I emphasized that success is not indicative upon having a father in a home.

I inculcated in her spirit that she was not inferior to anyone because her father wasn't actively involved in her life. I did my best to point out positive male role models when I met them. I explained to her that it was not the size of their wallets that made them good men, but the size of their hearts; it wasn't how they decorated their bodies that made them noble, it was how they adorned their minds.

I also helped her to understand that her father was not one hundred percent monster. He was a product of cause and effect like everyone else. He deserved our prayers despite his transgressions. I told her to focus on the good things she saw him do. Believe always that he could become a better man. Judging him wasn't going to make her feel better or solve any of her problems.

It's important that you make peace about the broken relationship you have with your children's father. If you are bitter about your divorce or separation, you must release your negative emotions. You must stop pointing fingers and blaming "your ex" for your problems. It's likely that he never put a gun to your head and forced you to be in a relationship. You must take responsibility for your choices and the role you played in the failure of your union.

Anger and pain are fraternal twins. This dangerous duo can literally destroy you and your children. It's a lie that time heals all wounds. There are people who spend their entire lives holding onto bitterness. God, not time, heals all wounds. You must ask Him to completely mend your broken heart.

"As long as you still feel anger and blame toward your former partner, you are actually still involved in a relationship with him." (Dr. Barbara DeAngelis)

I cannot say that the absence of a positive male figure in the home did not have various effects on my daughter's life. However, growing up in a single-parent home did not make her a failure. These effects are not life-threatening and they do not dominate her life. She has been able to do extraordinary things despite never having a close relationship with her father or ever getting significant financial support from him. We both believe that some issues just take longer to iron out than others and so that is what we're committed to working on every day of our lives. We continually pray for her father and hope the best for him.

Beloved sister, my hope for you and your children is that you live in peace. It would be great if you got married to an honorable man who would love your children as his own. I know that single parenting is not God's original blueprint for the family, but becoming obsessed with getting a man will only make matters worse. You cannot try to replace God with a man—it simply won't work. You cannot neglect your children while trying to find someone to rescue you.

Moreover, relationships are doomed to fail if you are not whole (committed to living for God). I constantly remind the young women I mentor that God must be a woman's main meal; a man is like dessert. Having a good man in your life can be a sweet bonus, but you can live happily without one. In fact, God desires that you have a man, but He doesn't want you to let a man become your idol—someone you will worship; someone who will replace Him.

"But You [God] have seen, for You observe trouble and grief, to repay it by Your hand. The helpless commits himself to You: You are the helper of the fatherless." (Psalm 10:14 NKJV)

Although desiring a husband is a natural aspect of being a normal woman, obsession with men and marriage can be spiritually dangerous. If we are lacking in any area of our lives, it is easy to become preoccupied with trying to replace what is missing. This desperation can lead to great pain and suffering.

God desires that we spend quality and quantity time meditating on Him. This doesn't mean that we completely abandon our dreams and hopes. It means we create balance and stability in everything we do. God desires that we have what we desire as long as it doesn't corrupt us. But our peace is disrupted when we spend a disproportionate amount of time focusing on who or what we don't have, instead of expressing gratitude for what we do have.

Wise and wonderful single mother, it's easy to make a man your god when you are desperate and overly consumed with fear of being alone. God knows you need help raising your children; He knows that you are a woman because *He* wired you that way. He designed your biological blueprint as a woman that created your natural desire for male companionship. However, God desires that you become totally dependent on Him for all of your needs.

"So many times…in our efforts to transform the men in our lives, we often forget about transforming ourselves. This is one of the most disguised and damaging ways we as women give our power away. We neglect our own process of personal growth, and thereby postpone our discovery of the magnificent feminine spirit that lives within each of us." (Dr. Barbara DeAngelis)

Even some women with husbands often suffer need; they feel lonely and incomplete sometimes, too. In other words, having a man isn't a guarantee that your life will be better than it is now. Being in a relationship is not a panacea for happiness. Instead of wasting time and energy trying to get a man, focus on being a better mother. Use the energy that you would bestow on a man for your children who are yearning for you to give them attention and love.

"True intimacy with another human being can be experienced only when you have found true peace with yourself." (Angela L. Wozniak)

It is imperative that you redirect your thoughts to God and fulfilling His purpose for your life. Regardless of your present level of personal achievement, there is always a higher place to go spiritually, mentally, emotionally, physically, educationally, financially, etc. (with or without a husband). Don't forget God created you. He knows every intricate detail of your personality and character. He is concerned about your needs and desires.

Contrary to what you have been told, the ability to get and keep a husband is beyond *your* power. You can't purchase a husband from a store. You cannot force a man to have a relationship with you. You cannot coerce a man to take care of his children if he doesn't want to do it.

You might be able to get his attention with your physical appearance, generosity, loyalty, and kindness, but even good attributes are not insurance policies that a man will appreciate you and treat you with respect. Beautiful and loving women get rejected, abused, lied to, cheated on and killed every day. You must learn to let God be your matchmaker. He knows what is best for you and your children. Remaining single might be in your best interest (for a season or permanently).

At the same time, if God knows you can handle a husband, you will not be denied. But, how can you wholeheartedly serve God when your sole ambition in life is to have someone replace Him? Moreover, if you are delusional about what marriage really entails, your days in holy matrimony will be short. Instead of begging God for a husband, ask Him to teach you how to be a blessing, not just to a man, but to everyone around you.

I never had peace about being single and knowing my child was fatherless until I surrendered my life to God. I accepted the things I couldn't change — the ones I couldn't force to happen. When I began to trust Him, I gave up *looking* for a husband. During this season of my life, I boldly went to God's throne about my desires. However, I was no longer frustrated about being single. My lack of male companionship did not equate a lack of love in my life. Remember, love comes *from* God, only through people. I accepted that my identity and self-worth as a woman, was not determined by my marital status.

The knowledge that God's love is sufficient can be hard for some women to grasp. Real peace is obtainable and will compel you to focus on enhancing your life through serving God. You will never discover how happy you could be during a season of celibacy unless you give yourself that gift. At some point in my own life, I decided that if it was God's plan that I remain single until my death, my life would not be less fulfilling. He had made me whole and stable; I would celebrate a life of peace and contentment with or without a man. Of course, I endured a few rough moments when I mentally got off track. However, it was during these times that I strengthened my relationship with God. At some point, I became comfortable with no longer having to know all the future plans for my life. I simply embraced the Planner, the Lord Almighty who is the author and finisher of my faith.

Talking to God about your problems is one of the most useful tool for becoming an effective single mother. I encourage you to seek Him for counsel, provision, and protection, but most importantly, RELATIONSHIP.

Some people are better authorities than I about *how to pray to get what you want*. I will never esteem myself a religious expert or theologian. I only know that regular communication with Him has been a healing balm to my spirit. Many religious people will tell you if you ask God for something, you can get it. Of course, according to them, there are stipulations you must follow; they will tell you that blessings are contingent upon certain actions. This is not my area of expertise. My only caveat to you: make sure you really know what you are asking for.

In the past, I asked God for things I didn't know would be devastating to my life. I couldn't see and know what the future held as He did. My lack of x-ray-vision didn't allow me to look beyond the surface of people and circumstances. I had to endure great suffering and get what I didn't want, to know I didn't want it. From those incidences, I learned to pray that God's will be done. I believe, with every fiber of my being, that God is willing and able to do what I request, think or imagine. I just don't concern myself with exactly how and/or when His blessings will manifest themselves.

If you are a single mother and struggling to cope with your marital status or lack of companionship, be encouraged. Amazing things will begin to happen for you and your children if you will simply trust God to provide all your needs. Don't fret about not having a husband. Start a life of uncommon peace by asking God to help you accept His greatest gift to humanity, Jesus Christ.

There is a Japanese proverb that I often reflect on. It says, "Better than a thousand days of diligent study is one day with a great teacher." I know no greater teacher than

Jesus Christ. Throughout my life I have examined the lives of many great men and women, but no single human being has inspired me more than Jesus. His teachings about living a life spiritually connected to God are incomparable to any I have ever studied. Above all, Jesus Christ is the greatest model for how to love.

Exert great energy and time to discover Jesus for yourself. Meditate on why He was given to us by God. God injected His preternatural essence into Jesus; this is our divine conduit that allows us to enjoy an eternal connection to Him. Of course, no one and nothing can save you, thus I am leading you to him who can—Jesus Christ. He is the only man you will ever need.

"Come unto me all ye that labour and are heavy laden, and I will give you rest. Take my yoke upon you, and learn of me; for I am meek and lowly in heart: and ye shall find rest in your souls. For my yoke is easy and my burden is light." (Matthew 11:28-30 KJV)

Lessons on Dating

In the following paragraphs, I share some thoughts about dating as a single mother. My greatest concern is for children who have no power to control their circumstances. Children don't have the ability and rights to move out and strike it out on their own when you have a man move in. Although there are men of character who are wonderful stepfathers, this country is filled with thousands of children (both girls and boys) who have been abused by their mother's boyfriend(s) and live-in lovers.

If you make the decision to date, please keep your children's safety in the forefront of your mind. Moreover, keep in mind that your children are emotionally and psychologically affected when they perceive that you care more about a man (who in most cases is like an uninvited stranger) than caring for them.

Date outside your home.

It's dangerous to bring a man into your home prior to having done everything in your power to ensure that he won't hurt your children. People are not able to hide their real identity and character for long periods of time. Therefore, pay close attention to how a man treats people. The way he treats others, is exactly the way he will treat your children.

Don't ever believe you are so special that you are exempt from abuse and violence. It would be wise to spend significant time with a man you're dating before introducing him to your children. I strongly suggest meeting your date in public places during the day, particularly during the initial stages of building your relationship. As you communicate, learn to spend more time listening than talking. What comes out a person's mouth reveals what's in his heart.

If a relationship becomes serious, give your children time to get to know a prospective "stepfather-to-be" before you make the final decision about the relationship. It's fair to give children several months or longer to get accustomed to a person in order to feel comfortable. Giving them an adjustment period reduces their chances of experiencing transitional shock.

Marrying a man who is a stranger to them creates a household of tension, especially for older children. Problems usually occur when children haven't had adequate time to get to know their "new dad." For blended families, the adjustment period needs to be even longer. People need some time getting to know each other before living together.

The statistics concerning blended families as well as second and/or third marriages are dismal. I believe people don't give children adequate time to establish and build a positive rapport with an adult who is expected to become their new parent. Moreover, they haven't had time to understand and mentally process how their new family structure is going to benefit them. They see a new spouse as a threat to their relationship with their parent rather than an asset to the family.

Additionally, children need to understand the shift in focus of the parent. Oftentimes when women who have children marry, their attention shifts to their new spouse. Some children feel slighted, even neglected. This creates resentment and anger among children making the home a place of chaos and turmoil. In their minds, their biological parent is giving someone else the attention for which they need and yearn.

Watch your emotional state when you're dating.
Many single mothers are looking for a man to help them pay bills and take care of their children. (Keep in mind a man may not be dating you for these reasons.) If you're in a state of desperation, you might compromise your values and/or the safety of your children. It would behoove single mothers to spend some time restoring their emotional and spiritual health before getting personally involved with men.

Make sure you've worked through any bitterness and anger about the divorce and/or break-up with your children's father. A sad and angry woman is so unappealing to a *good* man. Taking a hiatus from dating is a temporary situation. You'll find dating more enjoyable when you're already healthy and happy.

Manage your time wisely.
Dating can be a problem if you're spending a disproportionate about of time doing it. If you're neglecting your children while trying to date men, you will likely

experience resentment and rebellion from your children. It hurts children when their mothers act like they care more about getting a man than nurturing them. If you date, find a way to do so without taking away valuable time for your children.

Motherhood is one of the hardest jobs on the planet. Children need positive attention and constant guidance. Remember, your time to set a foundation in character is limited. You will never be able to recapture lost moments. How you treat your children during crucial developmental phases of their lives will impact your future relationship with them.

Decide who's more important: your children or the man (or men) you're dating. You are making a statement about what or who you value by the use of your time. There are only twenty-four hours in a day. Since most single mothers work, they have very few hours left to interact with their children. If you are going to use your abbreviated time to date men, you cannot be surprised when your children start to seek out other people for attention, love, and validation. Is this what you want to happen?

Chapter Twelve
Trust God for His Provision

"Being a full-time mother is one of the highest salaried jobs in my field, since the payment is pure love."
--Mildred B. Vermont

Reflection Questions

1. What is your attitude about money?
2. Are financial woes robbing your peace and joy?
3. Are you teaching your children that their self-worth and identity are connected to their socioeconomic status?

Just in case you don't already know, I am not a professional financial advisor. It's important to note that in this chapter, **I do not offer financial advice, but strategies that help you stop worrying about money. I decided to share these reflections about money because I personally understand how financial concerns can pervade our minds and have the potential to steal our peace and joy.**

Many single mothers face financial challenges and it's difficult not to let the spirit of fear consume us when we are solely responsible for every aspect of a household, especially without monetary support from the missing parent. I can relate to women who endure stressful jobs just to ensure their children will have their basic needs. They go to work when they are tired and sick in order to make ends meet. The idea that they are one paycheck away from homelessness is always lurking in their hearts.

My prayer is that you will evaluate your attitude and values about money. If you determine that money concerns are spiritually paralyzing you, let God help you adjust your thoughts about money in order to experience a life of genuine happiness. Walking with Him allows you to remain strong regardless of the balance of your bank account. Believe that God will not forsake you and your children.

It is likely you have met people who have very little money, yet seem content and grateful. On the other hand, we all know people who are blessed with much, yet they are tormented with discontent. They cannot sleep at night because their minds are preoccupied with the acquisition of wealth. After interacting with people in both groups, I finally concluded that both poverty and prosperity are states of mind. Both rich and poor people die. Rich and poor people get sick. Rich and poor people experience both gain and loss. Rich and poor people endure the same emotions. Rich and poor people laugh and cry.

"Money is an excellent servant but a terrible master." (P. T. Barnum)

Although money is necessary for sustaining your life, it achieves only one task: it solves financial problems. Money will not make you happy; it cannot save your or your children's lives; and it has limitations to what it can buy. Here is a simple truth that you should never forget: some situations cannot be altered regardless of how much money a person has. I have never seen money raise someone from the dead.

"He that is of the opinion money will do everything may well be suspected of doing everything for money." (Benjamin Franklin)

There are millionaires who suffered and died with great pain while discovering that their money couldn't save them. On the other hand, there are penniless people who triumphed over life-threatening maladies because of their priceless faith in the healing power of God. As a single mother, you must decide on whom (or what) you will depend. Will it be money or Jesus?

"Let your conduct be without covetousness: be content with such things as you have. For [Jesus Christ] has said, 'I will never leave you nor forsake you.' So we may boldly say: 'The Lord is my helper: I will not fear. What can man to do me?'" (Hebrews 13:5-9 NKJV)

One of God's greatest blessings to us is peace. This peace will forever evade us if we allow thoughts of money to dominate our minds. Whenever we spend a disproportionate about of time and energy focused on something, we are flirting with idolatry. God knows exactly what you need. He wants you to have money, but He doesn't want money to become a god in your life.

"Now godliness with contentment is great gain. For we brought nothing into this world, and it is certain we can carry nothing out. And having food and clothing, with these we shall be content. But those who desire to be rich fall into temptation and a snare, and into many foolish and harmful lusts which drown men in the destruction and perdition. For the love of money is a root of all kinds of evil, for which some have strayed from the faith in their greediness, and pierced themselves through with many sorrows." (I Timothy 6:6-10 NKJV)

As you strive for more peace about your financial situation, examine your heart. Are you denying yourself (and your children) access to God's peace because you're constantly worrying about money? Are you projecting these fears onto your children and making them feel inferior because of their socioeconomic status?

Wise and wonderful mother, you must petition God to help you release the thinking of the *world* which propagandizes that you are only as valuable as what you have, and that the ultimate achievement in life is popularity, prestige, power, and possessions. Perhaps it is time that you rethink these ideas. The following affirmations will help you embrace a life of contentment whether you are monetarily rich or financially challenged. (The affirmations are in no particular order.)

Affirmation 1: I will trust in God who has an infinite supply of all the money I need.

Worrying about money isn't going to change your financial situation. Make your needs and desires known to God. He will begin to reveal wisdom about financial resources and/or adjustments you need to make in order to improve your situation. Keep in mind that God is not a magician. Money doesn't instantly fall from the sky. Yes, I have received surprise checks in the mail, unexpected bonuses, etc.., but I have learned the hard way that I have to do *my part* in transforming my finances by learning how to budget, save, cut back and bring in extra money.

"Anxiety in the heart of [woman] causes depression, but a good word makes it glad." (Proverbs 12:25 NKJV)

Affirmation 2: I will teach my children that their worth is not determined by their socioeconomic status.

Having more material possessions than other people doesn't make anyone better someone else. If they have less, it doesn't mean they are inferior to anyone else. It is not good to connect your self-worth to what you can buy. Owning an expensive item doesn't make you more valuable.

God is less concerned about what's in your closet or garage, and more interested in how you clothe your heart. You deserve the best, but be careful not to associate the cost of an item with its quality. In many cases, there is absolutely no difference between the designer item and one that costs hundreds (or thousands) less except the label — the name on the item. Furthermore, more expensive items don't have special features: they can be lost, stolen, and destroyed just like inexpensive ones. Companies spend millions of dollars trying to convince you that you would feel better if you bought something more expensive. If you believe that you're in serious trouble.

When your primary focus in life is material gain, you become a slave to consumerism. Sadly, as you stockpile "things", the owners of the businesses you patronize stockpile money. The businessmen remain rich as you remain poor. (Are you working for things or to help others?)

"A good name is to be chosen rather than great riches, loving favor rather than silver and gold." (Proverbs 22:1 NKJV)

If you've got money to blow, more power to you. (Yes, there are people who can throw money away and never suffer a financial need or desire.) However, if you know you only have three dollars to put in your $300.00 handbag, ask yourself if that makes sense.

Finally, begin to think about who decides if something is valuable? Is a shiny stone from the ground really valuable or did someone place a value on it in order to make money? It's interesting that for thousands of years various groups of people treated gold and stones from the earth's core as if they were dirt. That's because they didn't place a value on those items. At the same time, shrewd businessmen discovered they could market shiny objects for a profit and become millionaires.

What's my point? You would have much more peace if you focused on building your relationship with God than trying to buy happiness. **Remember, money only solves financial problems; it cannot fix everything in your life.** In other words, if you had all the money you thought you needed it still wouldn't be enough to prevent sickness, death, problems, etc. Therefore, learn to view money with the right perspective.

Affirmation 3: I will be content no matter what my financial status is.

It's mentally healthy to meditate on what you do have rather than what you do not. I personally know people who are miserable because they are preoccupied with what they don't have. They constantly complain and gripe about what's wrong in their lives. Most of the time money—namely, not having enough to do this or that, is at the center of their wining sessions. Learn to send praises up to God rather than murmurs and moaning in spite of your financial situation.

Affirmation 4: God doesn't love me less than anyone else because I have less money.

Contrary to what you might hear, your actions alone don't determine your financial situation. There are so many variables, many beyond our control, working in our lives every day. There are people who work hard, give generously, and pray for success, yet these actions are not guarantees that they will become rich.

Nevertheless, don't let anyone convince you that you are loved less by God because you don't have tons of money. No human knows everything God is thinking. No human can rationalize why things happen the way they do. Instead of focusing on why you aren't rich, concentrate on doing rich things despite your finances.

"The rich and poor meet together: the Lord is the maker of them all." (Proverbs 22:2 NKJV)

Affirmation 5: My children and I are blessed and highly favored by God regardless of what's in my bank account.

Some people believe what people have is indicative of how blessed they are. Additionally, they believe a person's level of wealth correlates to his/her level of faith. I have seen people depressed because they thought God didn't bless them with material things because of His displeasure. Ask yourself where this message is coming from. Is this message devised from religious propaganda or the truth? Who determines how blessed you are—God or men?

"For [God] makes His sun rise on the evil and on the good, and sends rain on the just and the unjust." (Matthew 5:45b NKJV)

Affirmation 6: I will not seek out quick rich schemes.

If you study the lives of successful people, you will discover that most of them worked hard over a significant period of time to attain their level of personal achievement. Additionally, they had to navigate through complex problems in order to improve their financial status. Don't try to run and hide from the rich treasures hidden behind your trials. There are thousands of people who lose money every day trying to "get blessed" while bypassing hard work. For most people, the only time you will find *success* before *work* is in a dictionary. **"There is one who makes himself rich, yet has nothing; and one who makes himself poor, yet has great riches." (Proverbs 13:7 NKJV)**

Affirmation 7: I will petition God to show me how my gifts can empower me to work for His kingdom.

There are many ways to attain wealth. What works for someone else, might not work for you. For instance, your friend might earn tons of money selling insurance, but when you try it, you fall flat on your face. Make sure that you focus on your gifts rather than what seems convenient and easy.

When you confer with successful people, pay attention to the principles they applied instead of trying to mimic everything they do. Just because they made money selling cosmetics doesn't mean that's how God is going to bless you financially. Of course, embrace the principles they applied to acquire success but discover your own gifts and ask God how to use them. Use them because you love God. If doors open, He will have His hand on the knob.

"A [woman's] gift makes room for [her] and brings [her] before great men." (Proverbs 18:16 NKJV)

Affirmation 8: My credit score is only important to the world. My heart's score is important to God.

I cannot reiterate enough that what you have doesn't determine your self-worth. While we live in a world that makes trillions of dollars selling things most people don't need, you don't have to be sold on the idea that you are less valuable because you have less.

Affirmation 9: I will live within (or under) my financial means.

One of the greatest causes of financial problems is people getting things they really can't afford. I have been in this rut and I learned that I am much happier when I am not entangled in the chains of debt. Debt creates a form of modern slavery. Instead of a people working to improve God's kingdom, they're merely laboring to pay bills. Continually seek out wisdom on how to eliminate or minimize your debt.

Affirmation 10: I will not compete with other people for social status. Life is not a competition.

The person who leaves Earth with the most money doesn't win a prize. It is exhausting trying to outdo someone else. Let it go and save yourself from so much heartache. Be mindful that many of the people you're obsessed with only have the symbols of wealth anyway. There are weighed down with bad debt and struggling to maintain an illusion of prosperity. Don't fall into that trap.

Affirmation 11: I will teach my children that financial gain should come from actions that do NOT oppress, exploit, and/or destroy people.

Don't envy rich people who got their money by selling products and services that make people feel good, but corrupt, distract and/or inhibit them from doing good. Teach your children **NOT** to gain money from the exploitation of poor, uneducated and oppressed people. Demonstrate how they can earn money from careers such as medicine and science, education, law enforcement, etc. that protect and build life rather than destroy it.

Affirmation 12: God wants me to have money, but He doesn't want money to own me.

Obsession with getting money will ruin your mental and emotional wellbeing. I have seen people become zombies, unable to sleep at night because they don't have money. Some people have even committed a slow or instant suicide due to money issues. I assure you that if money is your master, you will be miserable. Sometimes when you have less, you have more—more peace, stability and sanity!

"Make money your god and it will plague you like the devil." (Henry Fielding)

Affirmation 13: I will emulate the life of my Lord and Savior, Jesus Christ. He did not live a life of excess and greed. Some people argue that Jesus was a rich man therefore it's okay to be rich. I don't waste time debating this issue. However, I strongly encourage you to **read the gospels for yourself**. According to the accounts (in the Holy Bible) of Jesus' life, He did not live in luxury, excess and/or greed. Carefully, note the primary focus of His ministry: man's relationship with God and people. Money was NOT a central theme of Jesus' ministry.

Affirmation 14: I will not focus on getting rich, but strive to do rich things in order to serve God. If wealth comes, I will remain grounded. If it doesn't, I will still be grounded. Seek God first and His righteous and everything you need will exist in your life. The right kind of wealth is a by-product of doing what you are passionate about. Furthermore, nurture whatever gifts you have. They will open doors for you. Keep in mind that God wants you to have money, but He doesn't want you to be obsessed about getting it.

Affirmation 15: I will be a cheerful giver. I will give faithfully, not foolishly.
    "So, let each one give as he purposes in his heart, not grudgingly or of necessity: for God loves a cheerful giver." (II Corinthians 9:7 NJKV) I cannot emphasize enough the value and joy of getting in the presence of the Most High God. He will give you wisdom and guidance about how, when, where and what to give.

Affirmation 16: I will not believe the lie that I must be financially rich in order to serve God's kingdom.
    Dr. Martin Luther King, Jr. and Mother Theresa are just two examples of people who didn't have tons of money, but they sacrificed their lives to serve humanity.
    "And whoever of you desires to be first shall be slave of all. For even the Son of Man did not come to be served, but to serve, and to give His life for a ransom for many [NOT MONEY]." (Jesus Christ, Matthew 10:44-45 NJKV)

Affirmation 17: I will not deceive myself by striving to gain the symbols of wealth.
    Ask God to give you the wisdom to emancipate myself from debts and liabilities. Some people want God to magically

erase the debt that they have created because of greed and hedonism. There is no question that God's compassion and grace supersede our sin. However, don't get frustrated if God doesn't behave like a wizard and you have to pay for your financial mistakes. He loves you even when He doesn't reward your irresponsibility, lust and greed.

"A [woman's] heart plans [her] way, but the Lord directs [her] steps." (Proverbs 16:9 NKJV)

Affirmation 18: I will not try to seduce a man for financial gain, and/or use my holy temple (my body) for money. Playing a dangerous game of Russian roulette with your body is irresponsible and selfish. Your children need you. Also, you must be an example of character at all times.

Affirmation 19: I will have integrity when I work. Although my job determines my salary, God will ultimately determine my income. I can testify that God can bless financially in ways you never thought possible. Let your faith work your patience. God's wealth is limitless. Don't let the fear of scarcity control you and distort your thinking.

Affirmation 20: I am not driven to work for materialism, but inspired by altruism. The principle of the harvest is true in nature and in the spiritual realm. We don't get what we haven't planted. The lack of money shouldn't stop you from serving others. Give your time and talents to others and so much more will be returned to you. When you give intangibles like love, hope, and forgiveness, they will be reaped from your garden.

"**Do not overwork to be rich; Because of your own understanding, cease!" (Proverbs 23:4 NKJV)**

Affirmation 21: I will seek God for wisdom about my finances. I will read books, attend seminars and listen to CD's that teach about building wealth the right way. I will learn how to use money, not mis-use and abuse it. Getting wealthy won't happen spontaneously. Knowledge empowers us to make good use of our money. Sometimes it's not how much money we make, but how we use it that counts.

Affirmation 22: I will not compare myself with others. Some people are born rich and some are born poor. I don't have to feel bad about people who came into this world with a financial head start. Again, it's so damaging to focus on other people's lives. The more you focus on improving yourself, the better you will look and feel.

Affirmation 23: I will wake up every morning with a sense of gratitude. I will express my appreciation to God for my blessings. I will meditate on what is right in my life rather than what is less than perfect. The power of gratitude is underestimated. Gratitude has the power to heal us spiritually and physically. Meditating on what we don't have sickens our minds and hearts. No matter what isn't perfect in our lives, there is always so much to celebrate. Shift your attention to the multitude of blessings that God has given you and watch your life transform with joy. (Purchase, my book entitled, *The Power of Gratitude: 365 Quotes and Scriptures for Healing Your Mind, Body, and Heart* for more inspiration.)

"Through the Lord's mercies we are not consumed, because His compassions fail not. They are new every morning; great is Your faithfulness. 'The Lord is my portion' says my soul, therefore I hope in Him'. " (Lamentations 3:22-24 NKJV)

Phenomenal single mother, you are not less loving, intelligent, beautiful, loyal, kind, generous, etc. because of your financial status. Poverty is an inconvenience, but it doesn't determine your character. If other people choose to judge you based on what you have and not for whom you are, that is their problem. Don't take ownership of their issues. It's not worth your time and energy.

Additionally, never compare yourself with other people. Some people were born millionaires and never had to work a single day in their lives — don't compare yourself with them. Likewise, don't contrast yourself to women who are married and have financial support from their husbands. You are functioning with one income and it's unreasonable to judge yourself because you don't have what they have.

Continue to consult God for provision, protection, and peace. He is willing and able to give you everything you need. Also, ask Him to reveal what adjustments you need to make with spending, budgeting, saving, etc. to do your part in transforming your bank account. He will lead you to the right resources and people to help you. That's right — faith without action equals no improvement. Smile!

Chapter Thirteen
Let Go and Let God

"Keep communicating the values you know are right but keep in mind you can't live your children's lives for them."--Felicia C. Hardy

Reflection Questions

1. Are you constantly harassing your children about what they need to do?

2. Are you trying to control every decision they make?

3. Are you leading them to Our Savior or are you trying to be their savior?

4. Have you accepted that you can't live your children's lives for them?

Good parenting doesn't make your children failure-proof. That seems like a no-brainer, right? However, many mothers respond to their children's mistakes unreasonably and disrespectfully. It seems strange since every mother has made her own mistakes. It's wrong to believe that our children will not fall just as we did (and continue to do) during various seasons of our lives.

Even when we have covered what seems like a thousand lessons on a particular issue, our children might still miss the mark and fall short of our expectations. When this happens, we must have the strength to be encouraging and supportive in spite of our fears, disappointment, embarrassment or shame. We must love them, anyway and teach them how to recover from mistakes with God's grace, compassion, forgiveness, and unfailing love.

The cutting of your child's umbilical cord was more than a physical act—a medical necessity. It was symbolic of all humans' requirement to transfer their dependency upon their mothers to total dependence upon God. Even though we benefit from a matrix of interdependent relationships, only God can be everything we need. No human being, not even a loving mother, can replace Him.

This does not mean that when we become adults we sever all ties with our mothers. On the contrary, we will always have a powerful spiritual connection to the special woman who brought us into this world regardless of the quality of the relationship. At the same time, we must live our own lives and let our children live theirs—so each of us can fulfill his/her own purpose according to God's divine will.

"Loving someone is setting them free, letting them go." (Kate Winslet)

The primary role of a mother is to lay a strong foundation in character when a child is growing up. Character will protect a child from needless heartache, as well as, equip him/her to serve as God's ambassador. Therefore, you must remember that every decision you make will directly affect your child.

Since you can never be perfect, it's paramount that you work diligently to make sure that the positive choices you make far outweigh the negative ones; this is a nonnegotiable aspect of parenting that must always be in the forefront of your spiritual consciousness. This is sometimes easier said than done because it commands an uncommon level of selflessness, knowledge, patience, and love that can only be generated through an unwavering and personal connection with God.

Also, as I mentioned throughout this text, the process building character is complex and involves a myriad of tasks.

Furthermore, our time to lay the foundation is limited. We can never turn back the hands of time so we must be mindful of everything we do, say and think. If we give our children a weak foundation, they will have a greater chance of falling quickly.

Keep in mind that as a mother builds her house, she cannot allow herself to become her children's god, and her children cannot become her idols. She must never forget that her children came *through* her, but *from* God. Each child is a unique being composed of a hint of a mother, a father, and a kiss of God.

"We must be willing to let go of the life we planned, so as to accept the life that is waiting for us." (Joseph Campbell)

A mother is assigned to be a steward of God's property. She should not try to control and dominate her children, but love, teach, protect, and nurture them so they will become independent, productive and God-fearing adults. Remember, mothers do not parent for themselves, but for God.

So often, banal forms of mothering actually involve being a tyrant and ruling children. When mothers try to make a child do and be things to meet their personal needs, they produce a depressed, unhappy and unproductive child.

"Let your children go if you want to keep them." (M. Forbes)

Throughout the years, I have taught children who are miserable because they cannot meet their mothers' expectations of them. They fall short of being their mothers' trophy or puppet. Instead of allowing their children to grow and become who they are supposed to be according to God, the mothers attempt to micromanage their children's lives. They never allow them to make choices for themselves. Sadly, they handicap their children from being able to take care of themselves and eventually their own family.

114

Wise and wonderful single mother, I know how difficult it is to let your child soar from the nest gracefully. If you are a loving mother, you don't want to see them fall and make mistakes. However, despite all your lessons, prayers and encouragement, children will still make their own decisions about what to do, with whom and where to do it. Some of your children's actions will make you proud and some will make you cry. Did we not do the same thing?

"Our fear is even stronger when we think we are responsible for others — our children, for example. We want to spare them pain, and so we forget to listen to the Sound of Creation. No one learns from someone else's mistake. If we respect others, we must recognize that they have a right to their own dance. Their own spirits will guide them." (Author Unknown)

Just remember to love your children at all times. Love your children when they do good things; love them when they do bad things. Love your children when they make you proud; love them when they disappointment you. Love them when they succeed; love them when they fail. Tell your children you love them every chance you get.

Love them and let them go because no matter how hard you try, it is impossible to rescue them from pain. They will never live a trouble-free life. Let God perfect His creation. If you haven't figured it out yet, you are not really regulating every aspect of your children's lives. Despite your noblest efforts to be an effective mother, no strategy you use comes with a lifetime guarantee. This is one of the reasons motherhood is so difficult.

"Truly loving another means letting go of all expectations. It means full acceptance, even of another's personhood." (Karen Casey)

Although motherhood requires greatness, the smallest things, many beyond our control, can skew the outcomes of our great love, prayers, work... for children. In other words, the time and energy we invest trying to build our children's lives can be destroyed easily by people and circumstances that we have no authority to affect. A relationship with God doesn't exempt us from facing trials and tribulations.

This fact should be neither disheartening nor alarming because having an authentic relationship with God means that all pain has a purpose. God is still in control, even when we are not. Every experience, pleasant or comfortable, has the potential to be an immeasurable source of inspiration as well as an opportunity for the manifestation of His glory and power **because God never wastes our hurt.**

I also know through personal experience and observation that there is a certain point in our children's lives when the role we play will change. From the moment they were born, they were trying to emancipate themselves as independent thinkers and unique beings with values and beliefs different from our own.

By the same token, children have the potential to replace the hard drive on which our lessons (both positive and negative) were stored. This does not necessarily have to become a problem. This is life — the way God has designed things to work. As children transition to adulthood, the mother/child relationship must change. The transfer of power, so to speak, is not always comfortable, and sometimes not easily accepted by both parents and children, however it will inevitably take place.

This does not mean that we will completely lose the relationship we share with our children; it simply means that as parents we must be willing to accept that our purpose and interaction are continuously changing. If you keep this in mind as your children grow up, your transition will be a little more comfortable, especially when we know we have fulfilled our duties and obligations.

As you continue the process of letting go, here are several powerful lessons to help you get an "A" in your parental transition. During the first wave of this process I was flunking the test when my daughter went off to college! I spent quite some time praying and crying while trying to regain strength and adjust to our "new life."

"There are things that we never let go, people we never want to leave behind. But keep in mind that letting go isn't the end of the world, it's the beginning of a new life." (Author Unknown)

Although I was so proud of my daughter and trying to celebrate her genesis of womanhood, it was hard accepting some of the choices she had made. I just continued to thank God that we are close and she felt comfortable sharing with me.

I learned to listen without judgment and let our "girl talk" direct my prayers for her. I continued to express my feeling respectfully. I coached her as I always had by reminding her that God's impressions of her far outweighed mine. I had done my best to raise my daughter with the fear and admonition of God. I had done everything in my power to set good examples for her, however at times I felt like such a failure when she revealed she had fallen short.

The truth was I couldn't control what she did. I had to let go and let God's grace and mercy keep her as they did me. The following lessons are how I finally got an "A" in letting go and letting God do His work in her life.

Releasing our children to God is an act of faith. We must trust that just has He protected us, He will do the same for our children. We made it and so our children will, too.

117

Lesson One: <u>A</u>djust your attitude.

If you think motherhood is about controlling your children, you need an attitude adjustment. Your children are not your slaves; their purpose is not to fulfill your will, but God's. Trying to manage your children's lives by forcing them to do things they know deep in their hearts is contrary to their divine calling will create tension in your child/mother relationship.

Give God His job back. Allow your children to feel powerful and confident by letting them make their own decisions. Don't get mad if they don't do what you want. Accept them as independent thinkers. You and your child are not conjoined twins. You don't share brains; you don't share hearts. You must live with the foundation you laid for them. Let go and let God.

Lesson Two: <u>A</u>cknowledge the difficulties with the transition.

When my daughter first left home for college, she thought I had gone wacko. I was checking in quite a bit. Since we've always been close, she candidly shared some of her experiences with me. I was trying to be objective and respectful, but I was going bonkers because some of my daughter's decisions were not reflective of what I had taught her — they were not reflective of me.

In order to save our relationship, I had to acknowledge to her that I was having a very hard time accepting this "new adult" person I barely recognized sometimes. I wasn't excusing my behavior, but I was trying to help her understand what I was going through. I promised to continually work on myself.

Lesson Three: <u>A</u>sk God for peace.

Knowing that my daughter had made decisions that were disappointing and potentially destructive disrupted my sleep for a while. Rarely do problems keep me up at night but I had a hard time reconciling some of her decisions. This challenging time in my life reminded me of my very limited control in the world.

Once again, I found myself praying more often and deeper. I just fervently petitioned God for peace until He gave it to me. I can't afford to let anyone, even my beloved daughter, rob me of peace. She is not my god even though I love her dearly. Wisdom teaches us to put no one and nothing above God, even our children. We can pray for them but ultimately their lives are primarily shaped by their own choices—something we cannot completely control.

"Whether our children are age six or sixty, we feel responsible for them. But often we carry guilt needlessly. It's important to realize that our children make their own choices in life." (Rob Parsons)

Remind yourself that your source of joy comes from God. When someone is having a bad day, you don't have to endure one, too. No one, not even our children, deserve the power to steal our inner peace. It's nice to celebrate our children's accomplishments, but when they fall short we can't crumble. We cannot ride on an emotional roller coaster with anyone. This is not healthy; it is spiritually and mentally damaging to have fluctuating feelings because of another human being's choices. There are times when I repeatedly say this affirmation: **"My joy comes from the Lord. I will let no one steal my joy."** I say this until I feel a calming peace encompass me.

"But without faith it is impossible to please Him: for he that comes to God must believe that he is, and that he is a rewarder of those who diligently seek Him." (Hebrew 11:6 NKJV)

119

Lesson Four: <u>A</u>dvise only when asked for counsel.

We all need good counsel but people can seem invasive if they are offering unsolicited and unwanted advice. At some point in our lives we get tired of other people telling us what to do even if we know we need help. The more you harass your children with your counsel, the more they will pull away from you.

It is natural for them to seek out independence. This makes them feel empowered and in control. Only slaves are not free to make choices. If you established a loving relationship in which communication is safe, your children will come to you for wisdom. Just make sure that you're not running on empty. Be objective and remain calm. They will think twice about coming to you for advice again after an emotional explosion. Get yourself together. Let go and let God.

Lesson Five: <u>A</u>ct like you're strong until you really are.

As a passionate person, my emotions can be very transparent. I had to learn to be less emotional as I discovered more things about my daughter. She is still a brilliant, beautiful, insightful, and spiritually conscientious young woman who I am blessed to mother. However, I am excavating dimensions of her personality that seem foreign to me.

We have so much in common, yet we have so many differences. I knew that whenever we conversed if she saw me get too upset, she might be reluctant to share what was going on in her life. I needed her to continue talking to me because our conversations would direct my prayers. Her words were a direct link to what was going on in her heart and mind. Today, I try to be cognizant of not letting my emotions go wild. I decided to fortify my inner strength. I will fake it until I make it.

Lesson Six: <u>A</u>ssess your feelings.

Introspection is so hard for us sometimes, but we must do it. Being our personal best means continually assessing our feelings. We must recognize the emotions that are pervading our hearts and appropriately manage them when we need to. This is the spiritual work we are called to do from the moment we are born until we take our final breath. We must never neglect nurturing our spirits.

Lesson Seven: <u>A</u>ccomplish delayed goals.

If you are a mother who decided juggling motherhood with so many other duties were too much, you might have delayed some of your personal goals. As your children transition to adulthood, this is the perfect time to go back and finish things you started. There is no better time than now to do some things you've always wanted to do.

Focusing on *you* will help you worry less about your children. Live your life and let them live theirs. Your dreams are not their dreams. Your goals may be different from theirs. Let them be and focus on you. Travel! Go back to school! Write a book! Start a new hobby! Read! Plant a garden! Walk. Get into you so your children can get into their own lives. Let go and let God.

Lesson Eight: <u>A</u>dapt to your new role.

As I mentioned already several times, mothers only have a limited amount of time to lay a foundation of character for their children. This time can never be recaptured. It is impossible to turn back the hands of time. The key to maintaining a healthy relationship with your children is adapting to your new role as confidant rather than caretaker. You have done your job. You've taken care of your children now it is time for them to take care of themselves.

Of course, they may still be in the nest getting their wings stronger to soar farther away. Nevertheless, you must adapt instead of setting a trap to snare them from realizing dreams and fulfilling goals. I just cannot apologize for reiterating the power of prayer because it works! Ask God to help you adapt to the myriad of changes that are coming your way.

Lesson Nine: A̱ssist, not insist.

I can't emphasize enough how trying to regulate your adult children's lives will create a host of problems. You are jeopardizing the health of your relationship when you act like a dictator in your children's lives. I understand that you have good intentions. I know you only want to help. Just because they are adults, they will not stop needing your assistance.

Keep in mind though that your job is to assist, not insist that they do everything *you* want. It's good to help your children sort through issues, especially when they ask you to help them do so, but the final decisions about important aspects of their lives should be made by them. They must learn to take full ownership of their choices and actions.

"Today I am amazed at the things our children have done and their wide range of interests. They are all living their lives and not the ones I would have planned for them. But I have learned that their lives are theirs, not mine, and in living their own lives they have given me experiences and an education I would never have had if I'd been fool enough to make them do what I thought they should do." (Bernie Siegel)

Lesson Ten: A̱ccept God's sovereignty over their lives.

No matter how things look, God is still in complete control of what's happening in our lives. If He chooses not to intervene during our trials and tribulations, He wants us to get powerful lessons from our experiences. Whether we walk in a dark valley of poor choices or reach the summit of our dreams, God is with us. He is also with our children.

We must accept that He works in ways we do not always easily understand. However, He is not less loving and less powerful because our children endure unpleasant, uncomfortable moments. He is with them at all times; we must continue to encourage our children to walk with Him.

Lesson Eleven: <u>A</u>ssume responsibility for your mistakes.

No mother is perfect. You are guaranteed to make mistakes. The goal is to make sure your good far outweighs the bad. If your children express resentment about your mistakes, don't justify or excuse your behavior. Assume responsibility for your actions. This is the first and most important step to emancipating you and your children from emotional bondage.

Confessing your sins is both spiritually and physically therapeutic. Additionally, it prevents people from using your sins against you. **"Confess your trespasses to one another, and pray for one another that you may be healed." –James 5:16a (NKJV)** When you make peace with God and confess your wrongdoing, it removes your shame and guilt. Moreover, it empowers you to lead others to healing. When you let go of secrets, you and your children can forgive and restore broken relationships. This is a powerful lesson you can teach them. Remember, you are still their most influential teacher. Demonstrate the value of assuming responsibility for one's mistakes.

So how many <u>A</u>'s did you get on your mother's report card? Give yourself a deficiency notice if you see some problems. **Take the first step towards improving your *new* relationship with your children by letting go and letting God reign in their lives without interference.**

123

Chapter Fourteen
The ABC's for Healing Broken Relationships

"Your task is not to search for love but to find a portal which love can enter." — Eckhart Tolle

This chapter was taken from my book, *Love Doesn't Hurt: Life Lessons for Women.* **(2012)** I have made some adaptations that might help those mothers who are estranged from their children and want to take the first step towards mending their relationships. Reconciliation is possible but it takes faith, courage, patience, and time. Children excommunicate their mothers for a myriad of reasons, but this usually happens because of un-forgiveness, resentment, and/or anger about abuse, neglect or hypocrisy that existed during their childhood.

The good news is that God is able to heal our memories and restore relationships. Someone has to take the first, bold step in this direction and it's commendable that it is you, the mother and leader of the family. While it won't be easy, it is worth the effort because there is a special blessing when mothers and their children are close. **People please God when they voluntarily work together cooperatively and harmoniously. God is about unity while our spiritual enemy is about dissension and discord.**

Blessed mother, be encouraged. Remain strong in the Lord and the power of His might. Seek His wisdom for the right way to lead in the healing and restoration of your family. God must first deal with you. He must excavate the toxic residue of shame, guilt and pride. He forgives you and now He must teach you how to forgive yourself.

Rebuke the tendency to trivialize, deny or justify any wrongdoing you've committed. Your children's perceptions

124

are their reality. They need you to address painful events in their childhood as well as take ownership for any pain you have caused. This is not about guilt, it's about acknowledgement. They couldn't pack up and leave as children when things were ugly so they expected you to protect them and prevent any harm.

Once you acknowledge your actions, people can focus on the future because they feel issues from the past have been resolved. God will remove the stains of your mistakes from your heart and replace them with humility and love. When He deals with a person's sin that person is free from ridicule and shame. What matters is that God has cast those transgressions in His "sea of forgetfulness". If other people want to re-hash the negative, remind them of your love, but let them know that God has already freed you of your debts.

In this chapter, I would like to share with you the steps I have used during my own personal journey of recovery and spiritual healing. For many years I was tormented by self-loathing, shame, and feelings of worthlessness. I was an emotional wreck who desperately sought out love in destructive and unhealthy ways. My inner troubles were so amplified in my heart that I could not move from human existence to abundant living.

It was not until I purposely sought out ways to heal my broken spirit, that I stopped blaming other people for my pain. When I committed to taking full responsibility for the quality of my life, I awakened a sense of immeasurable peace inside of me. Being in control of my own emotions, attitude and thoughts empowered me. Using my gift of choice allowed me to become better instead of bitter about my past. While I recognized my experiences had influenced how I thought about myself and others, I also recognized that the final outcome of my life would not be decided by someone who fails to love me and treat me with respect.

On the other hand, blaming people for my problems emotionally and spiritually paralyzed me. Taking ownership of my problems meant I had to adjust my emotional dependency on other people for my happiness. This allowed me to become victorious rather than waddle in my pain as a victim of abuse.

I discovered that the only path to spiritual wholeness comes from an intimate relationship with God, the eternal source of all good—love, wisdom, joy, peace... I accepted that God's divine blueprint for my life was perfect even though it entailed unpleasant and comfortable moments. Even the abuse I endured during various seasons in my past had a purpose. It did not destroy me; it did not prevent me from living a full life.

I cannot say that God causes pain. I do believe, though, He allows it; He uses it to create sparks of activism within us. My view of God is not negative because He does not always intervene in human affairs and rescue me from unpleasant experiences. I understand that all pain has a purpose.

While some people spend countless hours trying to explain and rationalize "why" people suffer—why things go wrong, I choose to accept God's use of both good and evil. **God is no less good—no less powerful, because He does not magically deliver us from all of our heartaches. Perhaps He knows that doing so would interfere with our spiritual development.**

I have not had a depressive moment since surrendering my life to God—to letting Him make decisions on my behalf. I do not worry about anything because my trust and hope is in Him, not in mankind. Nothing can interfere or stop whatever God wants (or does not want) for me. I would not appreciate the peace I enjoy today if I had never known chaos. I would not have my level of gratitude for God's unconditional love if I had never felt unloved.

Beloved mother, if your heart is broken know that God is the best doctor you will ever have. You are fearfully and wonderfully made by Him and He knows exactly what to prescribe for your healing. Go to Him through prayer and ask for His guidance. He is ready and able to teach you how to use your pain for a purpose. Release all of your feelings and hidden thoughts to God. Petition Him to teach you how to listen to the spiritual messengers He will send to you for wisdom. Most importantly, pray to receive the lessons that will heal your heart.

On the next few pages, I offer 26 ways to start the healing process. Try not to limit yourself with a strict timetable as you begin to implement these suggestions. Take your time and move at a pace that is best for you. Be still and let God work. God wants to heal you so you can be a source of inspiration and hope to other people.

The ABC's for Healing Broken Relationships

Apologize.

Tell the people you have hurt that you are sorry. Do not add the word, *but*, to your apology. **Do not trivialize, deny, or justify your wrongdoing.** Ask them to share ways you can help them. Listen intently. When you apologize due to remorse, you liberate yourself from guilt. If people refuse to accept your apology, it is their problem, not yours. Do what is right. Untold blessings come when you are found blameless. Resolve to live and let live. Remember, never trivialize, justify or deny any wrongdoing you have committed against others. Apologize to your children if you abused them, whether it was done intentionally or due to ignorance. After you acknowledge your actions, get everyone to agree to focus on a bright future, not the dark past.

127

Believe.

Believe that healing is possible with God's grace no matter how terrible things were in the past. Believe that God can heal bad memories. Believe that you can recover from your mistakes. Believe that you are a beautiful vessel made by God. Believe in the infinite power to become the best person you can. Believe that there are good people in the world who will love you unconditionally. Believe that God will allow broken relationships to be restored with beauty and love. Believe that God will give you the strength, knowledge and courage to transform your life.

Comfort the people you have hurt.

Estrangement usually happens because people are hurting. While you cannot reverse the past, you can assure people that you are sincerely sorry for any pain you (intentionally or inadvertently) caused. Focus on comforting them and letting them know that you would like a brighter future with them. Ask them to articulate what actions you need to take for reconciliation. Don't condemn them for their feelings, but don't let yourself be condemned. Focus on healing, not the hurt.

Do something you always wanted to do.

Take some time to do something with the people with whom you are trying to build healthy relationships. You and your children can heal by doing something you always wanted to do. Start small, but remember to believe in infinite possibilities that God can create. Do things that add value to character to all members of your family. Do things that build, support and nurture each other.

When we take the focus off our pain and honor ourselves with the right attention, our lives are likely to become more productive and fulfilling. Replace bad memories with good ones.

Don't make excuses about why you *can't* do something. Petition God, Your Divine Creator, to give you direction and wisdom. Expect great things to happen! Faith makes it possible, not necessarily easy. Excuses are the tools necessary to build a life of unnecessary failure. Do you want that?

Encourage other people.

This is one of the most empowering you can take to heal yourself. Think about what you have overcome. In order to maintain your strength, position yourself to encourage someone else. Being a positive source of human light and sharing uplifting words is painless and free. As God inculcates wisdom in your heart, He will give you an opportunity to share His revelations and truth with others. Don't be invasive; allow God to lead you to the people He has called you to help. Ask God to teach you how to speak without judgment and condemnation. You will be inspired to stay out of your abusive situation in order to become an example for others. Confront your fear of being embarrassed. Just do it!

Forgive.

Forgiveness is required by God. God forgives us and if we are reflections of Him, we must forgive others. Nevertheless, it is still difficult to achieve, especially if we don't know how to manage bad memories. While many people recognize forgiveness as a beautiful ideal, they spend their entire lives holding grudges and never pardoning themselves or others.

As they replay the offenses in their minds, forgiveness seems impossible and so frightening to them that they refuse or give up trying to do it. Therefore, I strongly recommend to people who are struggling with forgiveness, to fervently pray to God. When we talk to God, He answers us in our hearts and instructs us how to sort through and release negative feelings. He reveals to us that the purpose of forgiveness is to heal so that we can enjoy a fulfilling and productive life.

God is not mandating us to have relationships with toxic people. In fact, He never called us to be someone's punching bag or dart board. However, God desires that we are not hostile or adversarial to people regardless of what they have done. He is a God of great mercy and compassion. Again, we must be whatever He is since we are His children; we have inherited His spiritual DNA.

Reflect on the words of the late Lewis B. Smedes: "Forgiving does not erase the bitter past. A healed memory is not a deleted memory. Instead, forgiving what we cannot forget creates a new way to remember. We change the memory of our past into a hope for our future."

We can all free ourselves from the shackles of inner turmoil caused by un-forgiveness when we make an unwavering decision to no longer hold on to negative emotions associated with the pain we have caused ourselves and/or that which was created from someone else's actions. We must resolve to let people (including ourselves) off the hook for wrongdoing. We must hold on to the lessons learned and let go of the rest. Even if we acknowledge the pain and the memory of the offense that will inevitably resurface, we resolve not to meditate on what has already happened — what cannot be undone.

The benefits of forgiveness far outweigh its opposite. First, we get closer to God. The more we seek Him out for comfort, the more of it we will have. He draws closer to us as we draw closer to Him. He helps us better understand ourselves and others. With His divine intervention, we learn how to use our energy and memory to focus on good things rather than the negative. This is what enables us to become stronger, healthier in every way, wiser, more peaceful, and more loving. There is no way to become whole without forgiveness. The weight of un-forgiveness wears us down and burdens us with darkness, mainly inwardly. When we express gratitude to God for what is right in our lives instead of what is (or was) wrong, joy emanates in and around us.

Lastly, never forget that God is in control. Everything that happens to us is for His purpose. We might not understand why we endure tribulation but God has a plan to use it for something good. When we believe this, we can let go and let Him deal with people. Let go and let God decide the penalty of their wrongdoing. **In fact, Jesus Christ taught that God will not forgive us if we don't forgive others. (Matthew 6:14-15)** Think about your own mistakes. Would you not want someone to forgive you for doing something wrong?

Step down from the Judge's bench and accept God's verdict. Sincerely pray that God gives them the same grace and mercy that He has given you. The bottom line is that no one can heal without forgiving people. Forgiveness does not mean that you are required to maintain a relationship with an abuser; it means that you decide to no longer harbor bitterness about what he/she did.

Give.

I often teach young people that **in life we don't often get what we want; we get what we give.** Whatever you give will come back to you. When you give love, it comes back. When you give joy, it is returned. When you give mercy, you receive mercy. When you give patience, you will experience it from others for yourself. Give good gifts to others, regardless of what they do to you. Distinguish yourself as a child of God by choosing not to be vindictive. Lastly, give your burdens and fears to God. Resign as supervisor of the universe and give God back His job. He will give you peace, hope, joy, love… God may not give you everything you want, but He will supply all of your needs. Give Him the authority to decide what is best for you.

Help the people you have hurt.

When you momentarily take the focus off you, you begin to transform your pain into purpose. You can help someone overcome what you already have. Helping others can inspire you to restore broken relationship; aiding others transforms your own pain into purpose. I decided several years ago that I would create one hundred moments of joy for every moment of pain I experienced. You move from victim to victor when you help others, especially those you have hurt.

Inventory your life.

Make a list of who is in your life. Use the litmus test to determine who should sit in the front row of your life and who should be led to the balcony. Who is helpful (positive) and who is hurtful (negative)? Love both groups equally but choose wisely with whom you will spend most of your time.

Some negative people like relatives and co-workers you simply cannot avoid. However, you can decide to separate their negative energy from your spirit. They must move to the balcony of your consciousness. Affirm that they do not have the power to determine how you feel. Remember, you can choose not to be a victim of someone's irresponsibility, immaturity, weakness, malice, and failure to demonstrate unconditional love. While you cannot control what others do, you can choose your response. You can make a decision that you determine you own level of joy, peace, love, etc.

Jot down thoughts

Keeping a journal is a safe, healthy, and cathartic way of releasing emotions without hurting anyone. Jotting down your thoughts (journaling) can also be an important time for personal introspection. As you read and reflect on your own thoughts you have a better chance to assess them. What's inside you will eventually come out. Unresolved issues create a myriad of problems as they are manifested outwardly.

Finding out what is happening in your heart will give you a chance to add or delete ideas and feelings that might be harmful to you as well as others. While God is able to help you *spiritually* see things, jotting down your thoughts gives you a *physical* picture of what's happening within you. Always pray about what is revealed as you journal. Ask God to repair your heart. When your own heart is healed then you can work to restore broken relationships with others.

Kick Bad Habits

None of us is perfect. There are always one or more dimensions of our lives that need improvement. Facing the truth and taking action based on what is true will empower us to overcome and rise above obstacles. Kicking bad habits isn't easy but with God, all things are possible. We must lean on Him for support. I know people who went through years of secular counseling to break bad habits, but it was only when they discovered the incomparable love of Jesus that the shackles of addiction were broken.

God is real and He wants to heal us and make us whole. He has created us to be more than conquerors. Our job is to surrender to His will and way — to trust in the power of His might. Simply put, we cannot do anything without Him. I can't take my next breath without the grace of God! Therefore, I certainly cannot kick destructive habits without His help. Try Jesus today and watch amazing things happen in your life.

Love

Love is the most essential force the universe. Love doesn't come *from* people, it comes *through* them. Love's

133

preternatural source is God, the Creator of the Universe. In fact, God is love and love is God. If we know God, we experience love. However, a life without God is one that will never enjoy real love. Love will always evade godless people. Love's imposters come from the world which doesn't know love—cannot produce it.

The capacity to truly love is only possible through a connection with God. Love is the antidote for every ill in the world. It is the most powerful weapon against evil. Nothing is greater than love. Therefore, when you find love (God), you can heal yourself and restore broken relationships.

Monitor your inner self-talk.

Be careful about what you tell yourself. Self-deprecating language will damage your spirit. The state of your spirit, will determine the quality of your life. I remember how I once internalized the negative things I was repeatedly told about myself. I did not understand that the verbal and emotional abuse I endured could be reversed. I simply accepted that the degrading things someone said about me were true.

What God says about you is the only truth. He does not create junk. If you were worthless, there would be no need for you to be on planet earth. Obviously, you were created for a reason—**to be used for His purpose—not abused or misused.** What you tell yourself has the power to either build your spirit or tear it down. Write down some positive affirmation about yourself. Say them every day, throughout the day. Make this a priority. This is an effective healing strategy that I personally know works.

Finally, **"If you don't see the good in you, it's because you've gotten into the habit of criticizing yourself. Now is the time to change that habit."** -Janet Bray Attwood and Chris Attwood

Notice what is right.

One of the most injurious activities to your spirit is meditation on what is wrong. I have been there and done that. However, I have learned that focusing on what is wrong in my life distracts me from celebrating what is right. Life will never be perfect. People are not perfect. Your job is not perfect. You are not living on a perfect island.

Moreover, how helpful is it to gripe and complain about what is wrong (imperfect) in your life? I bet there is a strong chance that for every wrong thing in your life, there are three right things. Remember to look for the message in the mess. Your life's imperfections are aspects of God's perfect blueprint for your life. Smile!

Open your heart.

If you are not receptive and open to change, it will never happen. Whatever you want in life, open your heart to receive it. If your heart is completely closed, even good things have no way of getting in. Open your heart to new forms of love, wisdom and joy. Open your heart to uncommon forgiveness and grace. Open your heart to restoration and reconciliation. Your heart is large enough to receive all the blessings God has stored up for you. Don't sabotage your blessings by putting your spirit on lockdown. Remember, there is no fear in love.

Pray.

Prayer is talking to God. Prayer is the most healing and therapeutic action I have ever taken to heal myself. Prayer is different from conversations with humans. Those are important, too, but when you talk to God you never have to worry about your inner most secrets getting to the public; you do not have to feel embarrassed about sharing whatever is troubling you. He is the best Confidant you will ever know.

There is no subject off limits with God. You can tell Him anything. He really does listen. The depth of His love for you is immeasurable. You free yourself of burdens when you talk to God. You can pray in any place and at any time. The best kind of prayer is when you are alone in a quiet place. Make sure that there is nothing to distract you — no televisions, no phones, no radios and no negativity. Remember to get deep (drop everything and enter prayer). See chapter two.

However, there are times when you need to talk to God while you are at your job, in your car, in a dangerous place… God is omnipresent so He is everywhere at the same time. You must never let a day pass without praying. Praying is just that critical to your spiritual health. There is no other path to real intimacy with God, but through prayer. As you speak to Him, he begins to reply with answers to every problem. As you draw closer to Him, He moves closer to you. The more you talk to Him, the more empowered you feel. This power begins to chip away your brokenness.

Finally, go to God and tell Him about your concerns, fears, dreams, etc. for your family, especially about the actions you should take for reconciliation. God listens to, and answers our prayers. He cares for us more than we could ever understand. Get quiet and listen to Him speak to your heart. He will direct your paths.

Quit blaming others.

This used to be one of my favorite pastimes. I wanted people to feel ashamed and guilty for hurting me. I wanted them punished for the various forms of abuse I suffered. I would constantly talk about other people's faults. I was attempting to uncover their evil, but I forgot how God covered my own faults with His love. One day I had a terrible repressed memory. I thought about how God had been so kind and merciful to me. I was reminded how He repeatedly covered my sins. I recalled how He did not let me die during my darkest moments of brokenness.

As I prayed (mainly complained) about my pain to God, He revealed to me that I was just as guilty as the people who hurt me. I was no different than they were if I continued to accuse and judge them. I was literally shaken with conviction to stop blaming other people for my problems. God showed me that nothing happened to me that He did not allow. My pain had a purpose. I decided from that moment forth, that I would create a hundred moments of joy, for every tear I had ever shed. I suddenly understood that the road to my *vocation*, teaching, was not a result of happenstance. My experiences were attached to my destiny. They had prepared me to empower young people to maximize their potential; to not let disadvantages and distractions stop them from being successful. I thanked God for changing my heart and reframing my thoughts. The more I thanked Him, the more painful memories He erased from the ebbs of my mind. Say the following affirmation three times: "I will no longer blame others for my pain."

When you take ownership of your thoughts and feelings, you are no longer weak and powerless to accomplish great things. You transcend from victim to victor when you determine that no one determines your destiny but God.

Although you can't control every experience that occurs in your life, you can choose your responses to them. As Joyce Meyer once said, "You can either be powerful or pitiful, but you can't be both." Make a choice not to succumb to the agony of someone defeating you — someone else determining if you can be happy or sad. Decide that you will liberate yourself from other people's domination over you.

Reconcile

For some people it is easier to hear and/or read about a miracle than it is to see and experience one up close and personal. Reconciliation, particularly after a tumultuous experience, is a miracle from God. The biblical stories of Joseph and his brothers (Genesis 37-45) and the prodigal son and his father (Luke 15:11-32) are just a few ancient examples of recorded acts of reconciliation in the Holy Bible.

However, the newspapers are filled with modern-day stories of reconciliation such as Mary Johnson who forgave and reconciled with her son's killer, Oshea Israel. Also, a well-known evangelist, Joyce Meyer often talks about forgiving and reconciling with the father who sexually abused her.

There are also thousands of stories (past and present) of men and women reconciling with God. One notable bible story is about what happened to King David after he sinned against God with Bathsheba. (2 Samuel 11) I cannot count the number of times that I have heard of people living their lives in darkness, but finally surrendered to the power of God's love.

Reconciliation is only possible through God's grace. It takes an enormous amount of spiritual energy. Most of the time, it never happens because it is dependent upon work from both (or all) people involved with tumultuous situation. Forgiveness can be done by a single person but reconciliation (re-establishing a relationship with someone who intentionally hurt you or a loved one) takes cooperative effort.

When we pray for people who hurt us—and forgive them, God will move on our behalf. Sometimes, it is His will that people restore broken relationships. He will use reconciliation for His glory and purpose. I am blessed to personally know the depth of God's desire to heal broken unions and reunite lost loved ones. If He did it for me, He will do it for you. Ask God for reconciliation if it is your desire.

Spend time around loving people.

God has some beautiful spiritual agents on planet Earth. Despite all of the negative reports in the news, there are some loving and noble people around you. As you pray to God for healing, He will lead you to people who see love as He does.

I am eternally grateful that during my journey of spiritual recovery, God sent people in my life who could teach me how to rise above challenging circumstances. These people were a part of God's divine plan for my life; our encounters were not by chance. God's love worked through human angels who accepted me with my faults and imperfections. They allowed me to be a unique creation of God. I could be an individual and not condemned because I had particular values and beliefs different from their own. I believe that all people are blessed with loving agents of light around them. **So often though, we are so busy trying to earn the affection and acceptance of those who do not love us, we do not see the ones who do.**

Trust God.

When you trust God, and let Him make decisions on your behalf, you discover a level of peace that goes beyond human understanding. Trusting God means accepting that He wants what is best for you, whether or not you know all the intricate details of a situation. Whatever He allows in your life has a purpose. You have an assuredness that nothing is going to happen to you without God's approval. **Trust means that you believe that God is always there. He is beside you at the zenith of your success; He is around you in the dark valleys**

139

of despair. When you trust God, you know that all experiences — even unpleasant ones, will work in your favor.

Remember, I can't say enough, God doesn't change life; He changes us. Trusting Him means that in spite of everything, you know that He still loves you; He's carrying you through it all.

I know it's easy to become discouraged when you face unpleasant, painful experiences beyond your personal control. However, God uses the problems that we face as powerful learning tools. Behind every problem is an opportunity for spiritual growth. Remember, your pain has a purpose. It's up to you to look for the message behind the mess.

Use your time wisely.

Generally, healing is not a spontaneous action. It takes time and intentional effort to achieve. In order to heal, you must pay careful attention to how you spend your time. Again, do not waste time blaming others. Do not waste time trying to convince people you are worthy of their love. Do spend time praying.

Do spend time around loving people. Do spend time telling yourself and others positive things. Do spend time seeking counsel from wise, righteous men and women. There are 1,440 minutes in a day. How are you using this time?

Verbalize how you feel.

Before I acquired emotional maturity, I would often suppress negative emotions. Eventually my sentiments erupted like a geyser at Yellowstone National Park. I couldn't express myself calmly and clearly, and would become an irrational and emotional wreck when I had reached my breaking point. However, I was considered disrespectful whenever I tried to articulate my pain or respond to insults and verbal abuse. At one point I became resentful and angry that I was expected to endure name-calling and put-downs without protesting.

Much later I learned that anger is only dangerous when we **act on it in destructive ways**. It is imperative that we hone good communication skills and tame wild emotions. No one hears us anyway when we are out of control emotionally. Moreover, we must leave the theatrics for a movie career. Although it is extremely important to be mindful of our speech, we should never suppress something that is nagging our spirit. The key is to release our thoughts and emotions with respect and calm. In healthy relationships people can verbalize how they feel without scornful or judgmental responses.

Practice telling people exactly how you feel; do so without accusation—do so in private and with emotional control. Use tact so that you have less to retract. If you never find a way to verbalize how you feel, you will be like a human time bomb. Eventually, all of your emotions will implode. Do not be afraid to let people know what is inside of you.

Always keep a part of you just for yourself. Always use respect. Some people cut off relationships when they cannot oppress and/or control people. If you say something they do not like or agree with, they cut all ties with you. Consider this a blessing. If you cannot have open and honest discussions with a person, a relationship is impossible.

Welcome positive change.

I believe it is almost impossible to separate healing from change. Change can improve situations, but it can also make things worse. In order to experience *positive change,* you must be open to receive it. Remember, how you think will determine what you do.

Change is generally uncomfortable because it involves the unfamiliar. In order to change, you must trust God. God is always concerned about your well-being. He will meet you where you are, but He is continually trying to help you reach higher levels of spirituality. When you welcome Him, you are welcoming positive change in your life. Some stress is optional. You have the power to determine the quality of your life. Investigate ways you can excavate the things in your life that are harmful, unproductive, and unnecessary. Petition God for the courage to let go of the people and things that cause problems and turmoil you don't need.

X-ray your heart.

There have been times when I looked beyond the outer layers of my heart and found a malignant, spiritual tumor that needed to be removed. So often, the by-products of selfishness, dishonesty, jealousy, deceit, etc. build into a hard mass of sickness that we unconsciously keep deeply behind the fear of facing the truth. The truth is that human beings are selfish by nature, and must have supernatural help to operate above this natural inclination.

Trying to be unselfish without God is like trying to lose weight without reducing your caloric intake. Some might do it, but the results are generally short-term. X-raying your heart means closely inspecting the core of your spirit. When you find a tumor, a by-product of selfishness, you must have it removed. Let God be the surgeon.

Introspection is an integral component of long-term spiritual growth and healing. Only with the highest levels of spiritual maturity can a person admit his/her mistakes. It takes an even greater level of spiritual level to positively work to improve oneself.

Yield to God.

Throughout the last few pages I have shared how healing and spiritual growth are directly connected to God. *Who is this God, you might be wondering?* The term, God, is used so loosely today, by so many different religious groups that it is not surprising that people, especially young ones, are confused about Him.

Religious leaders with various spiritual doctrines, all proclaim that their way is the right way and the only way to God. Collectively, several groups of people have spent millions of dollars and billions of minutes trying to prove that they are right and all the others are wrong. To make matters worse, when religious leaders interpret their texts, their followers often get a combination of personal interpretation and literal meaning.

It saddens me greatly that children are the greatest casualties of these religious wars. They cannot figure out who to trust. Their parents expose them to one particular teaching, but the people next door, teach something else. God, amazingly, is often left out of the teaching! God gets lost in people's personal ambitions. So, for clarification when suggest yielding to God, please note that I am referring to the Creator of the entire universe.

God, a preternatural source of power, is the indisputable Creator of the planets that *man* (humankind) has yet to see; the sun that man will never touch and the millions of life forms that man will never completely identify.

Anything man makes has the potential to break down. Our cars, houses and computers are all made by man. Man, trying to be God, has spent untold fortunes trying to clone animals and humans, namely his selfish idea of perfection. But mankind will never be able to duplicate the moon.

And, no matter how hard man tries to forget, God always reminds humans of their finite power; people will die and there is nothing they can do about it. God, on the other hand, is the Eternal One. He will never die. He has been around for quadrillion light years before man, and He will be here long after man destroys himself. Yield to this God. Trust in Him. Get to know Him for yourself; do not merely take my word for it. He will guide you to the people, places and resources to ameliorate your spiritual life. He has been waiting to envelop you with His awesome love and power. Focus less on religious rituals and more on nurturing a relationship with Him and watch your life transform!

Zoom in on self-love.

You have probably heard the expression: "If you do not love yourself, no one else will." This could be one of the biggest spiritual fallacies known to mankind. It *is* possible for people to be loved by others even when they do not love themselves. Nevertheless, what is true is **that if you do not know what love is, you will not recognize it when it is being expressed.** In fact, you might even reject pure agape love because it is so unfamiliar to you.

Self-love is important because it removes your dependency on other people for your personal happiness. When you love yourself, you are no longer pre-occupied with trying to *find* it. Here are some facts to remember for life: people cannot *make* you happy. They are incapable of supplying all of your needs because they are imperfect; they make mistakes; they are complex. When the quality of your life is *totally* dependent upon other people, what is going to happen when they inevitably do something wrong? When you place unreasonable expectations on people, you make both them and you miserable.

Your spiritual needs must be deep inside yourself. That way when someone is having a bad day, you will not; when someone is depressed, you won't need to take a painkiller!

Powerful mother, God wants to heal you from the effects of broken relationships. Seek Him out for wisdom, peace and most importantly, His everlasting love. God is able to transform your life in amazing ways that stretch far beyond what you could envision or think. Will you let Him?

"And Jesus went about all Galilee…and healing all kinds of sickness and all kinds of disease among the people. Then His fame went throughout all Syria; and they brought Him all sick people who were afflicted with various diseases and torments, and those who were demon-possessed, epileptics, and He healed them." –Matthew 4:23-24 (NKJV)

Chapter Fifteen
Inspirational Quotes and Scriptures for Mothers

☼ "A mother is…one who can take the place of all others, but whose place no one else can take." (G. Mermillod)

☼ "A mother is not to be compared with any other person — she is incomparable." (African proverb)

☼ "Give a little love to a child and you get a great deal back." (John Ruskin)

☼ "My job is to take care of the possible and trust God with the impossible." (Ruth Bell Graham)

☼ "Do not be anxious about anything, but in everything by prayer and petition, with thanksgiving, present your requests to God." (Philippians 4:6 NIV)

☼ "Childhood does not determine an individual's destiny. However, it lays a foundation for every aspect of a person's life." (James Robinson)

☼ "There is just a sense of security that allows you to take risks. People think that it comes from wealth or generations of access and success, but it doesn't. The security of your parents' love really gives you the foundation to think you can fly. And then you do." (Michelle Obama)

☼ "Being a single mother is not a death sentence to your children's well-being. Throughout history women have successfully raised children alone." (C. Chérie Hardy)

☼"A man is who his mother makes him to be." (Ralph Waldo Emerson)

☼ "When people throw stones at you don't fight back. Use the stones to build your foundation [to do something great]." (Robert Ngatia)

☼ "We mothers, whether biologically blessed with children or having children placed in our lives by other means, must remember that we can't afford to give ourselves totally away. Something must be left in reserve for the nurturer." (Serita Jakes)

☼ "Every wise woman buildeth her house: but the foolish plucketh it down with her hands." (Proverbs 14:1 KJV)

☼ "Remember, when your child has a tantrum, don't have one of your own." (Dr. J. Kuriansky)

☼ "…The effectual fervent prayer of a righteous man [or woman] availeth much." (James 5:16b KJV)

☼ "It is the home that the child learns the basic principle of accountability for actions: first to those around him, and ultimately to God." (Maxine Hancock)

☼ "All that I am or hope to be, I owe to my angel mother." (Abraham Lincoln)

☼ "The family was ordained by God that children might be trained up for himself; it was the first form of the church on earth." (Pope Leo XIII)

☼ "Keep communicating the values you know are right but keep in mind you can't live your children's lives for them." (Felicia C. Hardy)

☼ "Of all the rights of women, the greatest is to be a mother." (Lin Yutano)

☼ "Mothers are really the true spiritual teachers." (Oprah Winfrey)

☼ "Who can find a virtuous woman? For her price is far above rubies." (Proverbs 31:10)

☼ "It is better to bind your children to you by a feeling of respect and by gentleness than by fear." (Terence)

☼ "God has a history of using the insignificant to accomplish the impossible." (Richard Exley)

☼ "Train up a child in the way he should go: and when he is old, he will not depart from it." (Proverbs 22:6 KJV)

☼ "Favour is deceitful, and beauty is vain: but a woman that feareth the Lord, she shall be praised." (Proverbs 31:31 KJV)

☼ "The real religion of the world comes from women much more than from men - from mothers most of all, who carry the key of our souls in their bosoms." (Oliver Wendell Holmes)

☼ "Don't let negative statistics pre-determine your children's future. God is an advocate for the fatherless. Stay with God and your children will amaze those who thought they were destined to fail." (C. Chérie Hardy)

☼ "Worrying is like a rocking chair, it gives you something to do, but it gets you nowhere." (Glenn Turner)

☼ "Pray for you and your children: sometimes that's all you can do." (Author Unknown)

☼ "Prayer is when you talk to God; meditation is when you listen to God." (Diana Robinson)

☼ "Pray as though everything depended on God. Work as though everything depended on you." (Saint Augustine)

☼ "Parents have expected the church to do what God has ordained the home to do. Remember that in order to keep the plague of death from our firstborn there must be a LAMB for every house, not every church. The church should only reinforce what is already being taught in the home. The church has the responsibility to equip parents to deal with their own children. The school system is not ordained to do that. Counselors are not ordained to straighten out familial problems. That's not the job of summer camp. We [ministers] cannot accomplish with programs what can only be resolved through love and parental commitment." (Bishop Dale C. Bronner)

☼ "It's better to give children a rule to break than to give them no rules at all." (Tipper Gore)

☼ "God always gives His best to those who leave the choice with Him." (Jim Elliot)

☼ "Children can stand vast amounts of sternness. It is injustice, inequity and inconsistency that kill them." (Father Robert Capon)

☼ "The heart of a mother is a deep abyss at the bottom of which you will always find forgiveness." (Honoré de Balzac)

☼ "Tell a child what to think, and you make him a slave to your knowledge. Teach him how to think and you make all knowledge his slave." (Henry A. Taitt)

☼ "There isn't a relationship in a family that is more important than the relationship a child has with her mother, or someone in that role, and we have to value that." (Michelle Obama)

☼ "I remember my mother's prayers and they have always followed me. They have clung to me all my life." (Abraham Lincoln)

☼ "Childhood experiences such as being allowed to try new and different things without fear of being told we're wrong or stupid, gives us permission to be creative and take risks as adults." (Julia A. Boyd)

☼ "…I've always believed that children are little adults, and at the end of the day, you have to teach them how to be responsible for their own lives. As parents our job is to take their power and use it in a way that is pro-life, not take all of our child's power to make them do things we want them to do." (Jada Pinkett-Smith)

☼ "Life affords not greater responsibility, no greater privilege, than the raising of the next generation." (C. Everett Koop)

☼ "Children will not remember you for the material things you provided but for the feeling that you cherished them." (Richard L. Evans)

☼ "Taking time for ourselves is not selfish; it's necessary for self-preservation." (Angela Burt-Murray)

☼ "When you are a mother, you are never really alone in your thoughts. A mother always has to think twice, once for herself and once for her child." (Sophia Loren)

☼ "Perhaps the greatest social service that can be rendered by anybody to the country and to mankind is to bring up a family." (George Bernard Shaw)

☼ "The future destiny of the child is always the work of the mother." (Napoleon Bonaparte)

☼ "Psychologists will attest that parents can program their children for joy and achievement with the words they share and the example they set." (Angela Burt-Murray)

☼ "The formative period for building character for eternity is in the nursery. The mother is queen of that realm and sways a scepter more potent than that of kings or priests" (Author Unknown)

☼ "Loving a child is circular business…The more you give, the more you get, the more you get, the more you want to give." (Penelope Leach)

☼ "The moment a child is born, the mother is also born. She never existed before. The woman existed, but the mother, never. A mother is something absolutely new." (Rajneesh)

☼ "Correct your son, and he will give you rest; Yes, he will give delight to your soul." (Proverbs 29:17 NKJV)

☼ "The rod and rebuke give wisdom, but a child left to himself brings shame to his mother." (Proverbs 20:15 NKJV)

☼ "If I could share one lesson from my battle with cancer, it would be this: We must free ourselves from the crushing and prolonged stress that can break down the immune system, leaving our bodies open to catastrophic illness. …It is not enough just to change the way we treat our bodies; we must change the very patterns of our thoughts. We must empty ourselves of the resentment and bitterness that could poison our cells, and let love, faith compassion and forgiveness rule in their place." (Yvonne Williams, an ambassador for the American Cancer Society)

☼ "Look for the good, not the evil, in the conduct of members of the family." (Jewish Proverb)

☼ "The Lord watches over strangers; He relieves the fatherless and widow; but the way of the wicked He turns upside down." (Proverbs 146:9 NKJV)

☼ "Being a full-time mother is one of the highest salaried jobs…since the payment is pure love." (Mildred B. Vermont)

☼ "Discipline your children with a desire motivated to protect them." (Dr. Charles Stanley)

☼ "What is the best parenting strategy for all children? It is unconditional love!" (Felicia C. Hardy)

☼ "Babies are living jewels, dropped unstained from heaven." (Sir Frederick Pollack)

☼ "It is easier to build strong children than to repair broken men." (Frederick Douglass)

☼ "Biology is the least of what makes someone a mother." (Oprah Winfrey)

☼ "Motherhood has the greatest potential influence in human life." (Author Unknown)

☼ "Making the decision to have a child is momentous. It is to decide forever to have your heart go walking around outside your body." (Elizabeth Stone)

☼ "A mother who radiates self-love and self-acceptance actually vaccinates [her children] against low self-esteem." (Naomi Wolf)

☼ "Our children are only lent to us. We never know just how long we are able to keep them for. So, kiss them. Cuddle them. Praise them and hold them tightly. But most of all…tell them you love them every day." (Author Unknown)

☼ "Raise your words, not your voice. It is rain that grows flowers, not thunder." (Rumi)

☼ "Mothers cannot give from a depleted source. Every mother needs emotional, mental, physical, and spiritual validation, nourishment, and support. When a mother is respected and well cared for, she and her whole family will benefit." (Author Unknown)

☼ "The goal of parenting isn't to create perfect [children]. It's to point [them] to the perfect God." (Lindsey Bell)

☼ "Parents are the foundation upon which children build their lives. When the structure of the foundation isn't stable, the foundation is weak." (Iyanla Vanzant)

A Prayer for Mothers

Dear Heavenly Father,

Thank you for honoring me with motherhood. I am grateful for Your presence in my life. I acknowledge that my children are blessings from You. I rejoice that they belong to You — that you are the true Author and Finisher of their faith. Heavenly Father, help me to be a righteous steward who will prepare them for Your kingdom. I thank you for helping me to the job with which you have entrusted me. I humbly submit to your will in order to be an effective mother. Speak to my heart. Give me a clean heart and put the right spirit within me.

Blessed Creator, I cannot raise my children the right way without Your wisdom and guidance. I need You, Lord. Please tell me what to do, say and think. Show me how to be healthy in every aspect of my life so that I can be a mother my children will honor and cherish.

Take away from me what I don't need. Put into me what I do. I will trust You for all things. I am grateful for Your love, compassion, peace, joy...Thank You for being there for me. Thank You for listening to me. Thank You for answering my prayers, according to Your will.

Lord, please protect my children. Keep them from evil. Reveal Your presence to them. Speak to their hearts, Heavenly Father. Teach them Your way. Let them experience Your mercy, grace, and love. I thank you for answering my prayers and keeping me and my children in Your care.

In Jesus' name, Amen.

Acknowledgements

Heavenly Father: I know that I could do absolutely nothing without you. I thank you for being my faithful Rod and Staff.

To my family: You are a reflection of God's unfailing love. I feel blessed to be connected to each of you in a special way.

Beloved Daughter: You've been an inspiration to me since the moment you were born. I pray this book will help mothers and their children have the beautiful relationship that we share. You are a blessing and one of God's greatest gifts to me.

To the Salvation Army, the first church I ever attended: You gave me my first Bible. Most importantly, you taught me (and hundreds of disadvantaged youth) about the story of Jesus Christ as an act of God's unconditional and unwavering love for mankind. For this, I am infinitely appreciative.

About the Author

C. Chérie Hardy was born and raised in Florida. She is an award-winning educator who has served in public schools for almost 30 years. She is also a certified life coach and inspirational speaker. Below are titles of some of her other literary works.

- *Love Doesn't Hurt: Life Lessons for Women*
- *Daily Pearls: Inspiration and Wisdom for Each Day of the Year*
- *The Power Gratitude: 365 Quotes and Scriptures for Healing Your Mind, Body, and Heart*
- *Encouragement for the Grieving Heart: 365 Uplifting Quotes and Scriptures for Coping with Loss*
- *The Orange Zebra (first children's book)*
- *The Orange Zebra and The Kind Giraffe*
- *Three Nights in December (first novel)*
- *Morning Chai with God: Inspirational Messages that Strengthen Your Faith*

Ms. Hardy is the proud mother of one daughter. She and her family currently reside in the Atlanta Metropolitan area.

Please feel free to send your questions and comments to: **ccheriehardy@gmail.com**

Notes

www.ingramcontent.com/pod-product-compliance
Lightning Source LLC
Chambersburg PA
CBHW070806280326
41934CB00012B/3081